Mimosa

Mimosa

The life and times of the ship
that sailed to Patagonia

Susan Wilkinson

This book is dedicated to the memory of *mintai Mimosa* – the Welsh men, women and children who sailed on her to Patagonia and with whom her name is forever linked – and to the doctor who accompanied them, my great-great-uncle, Thomas Greene.

First impression: 2007
© Susan Wilkinson and Y Lolfa Cyf., 2007

The publishers wish to acknowledge the financial support of
Cyngor Llyfrau Cymru.

Cover design: Y Lolfa

ISBN: 9 780 86243 9 521
ISBN: 0 86243 952 3

Printed on acid-free and partly recycled paper
and published and bound in Wales by
Y Lolfa Cyf., Talybont, Ceredigion SY24 5AP
e-mail ylolfa@ylolfa.com
website www.ylolfa.com
tel 01970 832 304
fax 832 782

Susan Wilkinson was born in India, grew up in Ireland and now lives in Canada. Her great-great-uncle was Thomas Greene, the doctor on the voyage to Patagonia. She is the author of *Sebastian's Pride*, a novel set in 19th century Argentina, and is a contributor to the *Buenos Aires Herald* and *Ninnau y Drych*. She travels regularly to Argentina and has been an invited speaker at conferences in Patagonia.

Contents

Illustrations

Alexander Hall & Sons shipyard office staff, 1862
(courtesy of the Aberdeen Art Gallery and Museums Collections)

Mould loft
(courtesy of the Aberdeen Art Gallery and Museums Collections)

Raft of Scantlings
(*The Deeside Field* by V J Buchan Watt, The Rosemount Press, Aberdeen,
1925)

Suspension Bridge at Aboyne
(*The Scenery of the Dee with Pen and Pencil* by Andrew Gibb, FSA, Gibb &
Hay, Aberdeen, 1884)

Robert Vining, 1874
(Courtesy of the Liverpool Record Office, Liverpool Libraries)

S.S. *Mimosa*
(Courtesy of the Parker Gallery, London)

Mimosa's China Voyages

Advertisement for the auction of *Mimosa*'s tea cargo, Halifax
(*Halifax Acadian Recorder*, April 12, 1856)

Michael Daniel Jones and Anne Lloyd Jones with Eluned Morgan,
daughter of Lewis Jones.
(Courtesy of Tegai Roberts, Gaiman)

Bill of Receipt for the Charter of *Mimosa*, 1865
(Bangor Manuscripts 11456, University of Bangor)

The Voyage to Patagonia, 1865
(*The Great Venture* by Aled Lloyd Davies, Welsh Heritage and Culture Project, 1987)

The Landing
(*La valle de la esperanza* by Carlos Bartomeo, El Ateneo, Buenos Aires, 1943)

The Last Cargo
(Liverpool Customs Bill of Entry, March 11, 1872)

The Final Entry
(*Registry of Transactions Book*, vol. IV, p. 512, Merseyside Maritime Museum, Liverpool)

Author's Note

In writing the story of *Mimosa*, the ship which, in 1865, sailed with the first Welsh settlers to Patagonia, I have attempted to find all substantiated facts about her, about the men who built her, who owned her, who sailed in her and about the period in maritime history which caused her to be constructed in the first place. This entailed reading articles and books on various aspects of history and maritime lore and writing to anyone who might provide a piece of the puzzle that would make up the entire picture of *Mimosa*'s life and times. Little by little, the facts of her life emerged, from her construction in Aberdeen to her last days on the mosquito-infested coast of West Africa.

Initially, my interest in her was purely personal, in that my ancestor, Thomas Greene, was the young doctor who accompanied the Welsh settlers to Patagonia. I knew nothing of the ship except her name and that her name was linked to a story that has made her almost a legend. It seems to be a strange phenomenon that, when one is interested in a given subject, facts somehow emerge and sometimes even drop into one's lap, increasing and augmenting one's knowledge and further stimulating one's curiosity. So it was with the story of the little clipper ship that gained immortality because of a voyage that was unique in the history of the world. A letter or email of inquiry, a chance conversation, a book on maritime history found on a library shelf all directed me to parts of that story.

Another ship called *Mimosa* also existed and is listed in *Lloyd's Register*. She was an iron ship of 541 tons, built in Liverpool in 1872. Despite the coincidence of two ships having the same name, there is not the slightest doubt that the one here described is the one which sailed to Patagonia in 1865.

The longest single part of the book deals with the voyage to Patagonia. Not only is there more historical documentation surrounding this one voyage, but, for many, it is the voyage that defines her. This was the voyage that separated *Mimosa* from other clippers, giving her an aura of legend that other clippers do not have.

Of the accounts written of *Mimosa*'s historic voyage to Patagonia only one exists of the day-to-day events on the voyage itself. This was the diary of Joseph Seth Jones, which was written in Welsh. It is held in the National Library of Wales in Aberystwyth, and it ends with the arrival and disembarkation at New Bay. Another passenger, Richard Ellis, also kept a diary. The entries, written in English, are brief, documenting little other than the date of departure from Liverpool and arrival at New Bay. Eighteen-year-old James Davies, travelling alone, likewise kept a diary during the voyage, which, according to Joseph Seth Jones who filled in gaps in his own entries from it, consisted mostly of the titles of the sermons given by the ministers on board. James Davies died six months after arrival in Patagonia, when he wandered too long and too far in the land of bush and thorn that stretched without landmarks from horizon to horizon, and his diary has likewise vanished. Other accounts, written by some who were also passengers, were written after the voyage, sometimes many years afterwards. My ancestor, Thomas Greene, also kept a journal of the voyage. Tragically, it was lost during his subsequent travels in South America. However, some of his experiences in Patagonia are documented in a letter published in the *Liverpool Mercury* in January 1866, two months after his departure from Patagonia.

Amazingly, all but a few of the crew agreements and official logs of *Mimosa*'s voyages to China, Brazil, and New Calabar in West Africa, exist. I have traced and obtained copies of all existing records of *Mimosa*'s voyages and 'runs' between home ports. Most are held at the National Archives in Kew. A few are held at the National Maritime Museum at Greenwich. One is held at the Liverpool Record Office; and the remainder are held in the Maritime History Archives of Memorial University, St John's, Newfoundland. A list of her voyages and 'runs' is appended.

I am neither a maritime historian nor an academic. I hope that those who are will bear with my limitations. I hope, too, that those who are Welsh will forgive the great voids in my knowledge of the historical events which led to the establishment of *Y Wladfa*. Like my ancestor, Thomas Greene, there is much that I neither know nor understand, simply because I am not Welsh. I hope, too, that they will forgive the liberties I have taken in describing those who, for one reason or another, decided to leave Wales and Lancashire for a largely unknown and desolate part of the world. Above all, theirs is a human story, and I have attempted to describe it in as human a way as possible as I sought to ponder the reasons why they decided to go to Patagonia.

There can never be an entire picture of *Mimosa*'s life and times. Pieces will always be missing. Incomplete as it is, this is my interpretation of her life and times and of her most historic and now legendary voyage.

David R MacGregor ends his excellent book, *The Tea Clippers: Their History and Development, 1833-1875*, thus:

> *Ship lovers do tend to concentrate their worship and interest in a few of the best-known ships and an attempt has been made here to widen the field a little. Without a doubt the forgotten names of other clippers will come to light and it will be interesting to discover whether any other record passages are unearthed.*

I hope that this book will help to widen the knowledge a little of what was, for some, the most noteworthy clipper of them all, whose name will never be forgotten, record passages notwithstanding.

Acknowledgements

There are so many people who helped me in my research; without them the writing of this book would not have been possible. They were all generous with their time and their knowledge, and I owe them all a deep debt of gratitude. I have taken from them what I felt I needed for *Mimosa*'s story, necessarily omitting much. Any mistakes or inaccuracies I may have made are entirely my own.

I am greatly indebted to Catherine Walker, Assistant Keeper of Maritime History at the Aberdeen Maritime Museum for many details on the Alexander Hall & Sons shipyard and for providing photographs of the shipyard men who were undoubtedly instrumental in *Mimosa*'s construction. To Eileen Young, Library Assistant at Aberdeen Central Library, I owe heartfelt thanks for providing fascinating articles on Glen Tanar, where the oak for *Mimosa*'s hull was obtained, and of Footdee, where the Hall shipyard stood. I also wish to thank Dr David M Bertie, Curator of Local History of the Aberdeenshire Heritage, of Peterfield, Scotland, for other aspects of *Mimosa*'s birthplace.

In London, I am indebted Stephen Freeth and Peter Ross of the Guildhall Library for helping me to access information on *Mimosa*'s various masters. Searching crew agreements and official logs of *Mimosa*'s various voyages was an onerous task; and I am deeply grateful to Barbara Kirkaldy for her thorough and painstaking research in accessing those held in the National Maritime Museum in Greenwich and the National Archives in Kew. The crew agreement and the official log of the voyage to Patagonia and the list of passengers compiled by Richard Berwyn are in the National Archives, Kew; and I owe thanks to Bruno Derrick for sending me photocopies of these. Thanks, too, to Dr Ifor James of the London Welsh Association for sharing with me his knowledge of 19th

Acknowledgements

century medical conditions prevalent on the voyage to Patagonia.

In Canada, I wish to acknowledge the help of Paula Marshall, archivist of the Maritime History Archives at Memorial University of Newfoundland, which holds copies of the crew agreements and logs of *Mimosa*'s voyages, following her voyage to Patagonia, copyright of which are held by the National Archives in Kew. Also in Canada, I would like to thank Garry D Shutlak, Senior Archivist of the Nova Scotia Archives in Halifax, for alerting me to information on the auction of *Mimosa*'s first cargo of tea; and the staff of the Reference Library of Toronto for their help in obtaining books on maritime history held in other libraries in Canada. My thanks go, too, to my husband, Hugh, for undertaking research at various archives when on his trips to London.

The Merseyside Maritime Museum in Liverpool houses the register of *Mimosa* as well as the three volumes detailing the many transactions relating to her changes of ownership. I extend many thanks to the staff, especially Lorna Hyland, Assistant Curator of Maritime Archives, for all their help. I am also indebted to port historian, Michael D Stammers, for expanding my knowledge on 19th century Liverpool and its miles of docks. The staff of the Liverpool Record Office assisted me in gaining access to information on Robert Vining and William Killey, *Mimosa*'s first and principle owners, and I am especially grateful to Roger Hull, Research Officer. My thanks go, too, to maritime art historian and writer A S Davidson for information on the painting of *Mimosa*, to Professor Peter N Davies of the University of Liverpool for details on Stuart & Douglas, *Mimosa*'s last owners, and to the Merseyside Welsh Historical Society, especially Dr Ben D Rees and Dr Arthur Thomas.

Without the help of the World Ship Trust, an international organization dedicated to the preservation, in all its aspects, of historic ships, much of the information on *Mimosa* might never have been obtained. I especially wish to thank Paul Ridgway for his help and encouragement; Eric Lawson, the Canadian representative, for directing me to many experts in various aspects of maritime history; and Paul Quinn of Staffordshire for sharing with me his considerable knowledge of hulks in New Calabar – *Mimosa*'s final fate and destination. I owe a great debt of gratitude to the late David R MacGregor for instructing me, during the brief acquaintance we had, on matters relating to the structure of clipper ships. I know that I sorely tried his patience by my ignorance of sail plans and clipper dimensions.

A portrait of *Mimosa,* executed when she was in her sailing prime, was held by the Parker Gallery in London, which specializes in maritime art; and I wish to thank its curator, Brian J Newbury, for answering my queries on the painting's whereabouts and for providing an authenticated photograph of the painting.

For genealogical information on *Mimosa*'s passengers who sailed to Patagonia in 1865, and their ultimate fates, I would like to thank Jeremy Howat of York. I would also like to thank Jean Debney in Berkshire for giving me valuable information on her ancestor, Rhudderch Huws, who figured so prominently in accounts of the voyage. Thanks, too, to Michelle Wilson of Vermont for giving me information on her ancestor, Thomas Kemp, *Mimosa*'s first master.

Most accounts of *Mimosa*'s voyage to Patagonia, especially letters written home to Wales by the passengers themselves, exist only in Welsh. My thanks to the Welsh-speakers I consulted who patiently translated excerpts of various documents, or explained their contents.

In Wales, I wish to extend my deepest gratitude to writer and historian Elvey MacDonald, a direct descendent of several of the passengers on board, for sharing with me his considerable knowledge of the events and aftermath of the voyage to Patagonia and for his steadfast encouragement over the years I spent in writing this book. Very special thanks to Ceris

Gruffudd of the National Library of Wales in Aberystwyth; to Eironedd Baskerville, also of the National Library of Wales; and Professor Robert Owen Jones of the University of Cardiff. Thanks, too, to Aled Lloyd Davies of Mold for initial information on the voyage; Huw Williams of Ystradgynlais for information on his ancestors, who were among *Mimosa*'s passengers; Dafydd Tudur of Bangor for his help in accessing manuscripts on the preparations for the voyage, which are held at the University of Bangor; Cathrin Williams of Menai Bridge for her hospitality during my stay in Bangor and for the wonderful conversations we had on our drives in the Llŷn Peninsula. I would also like to thank Dr Dewi Evans of the Department of Welsh at University College, Dublin, for additional background information on the Welsh Colony in Patagonia.

In Argentina, I wish to thank Tegai Roberts, Curator of the Museo Regional in Gaiman for giving me so much of her time and her knowledge of *Y Wladfa,* and especially for data on her great-grandfather, Michael D Jones; Luned Roberts de González, OBE, also of Gaiman, for the generosity of her hospitality over the years at *Plas y Graig;* Dr David Williams and Ansel René Davies of Trelew for giving me access to the private biographies each has compiled on their ancestors, who were among *Mimosa*'s passengers to Patagonia; the late Doris ap Iwan de Deane of Buenos Aires for her reminiscences of her grandmother, Anne Lloyd; Fernando Coronato of the Centro Estudios Históricos y Sociales of Puerto Madryn; Patricia and Alan Mackern for their generous hospitality during my stays in Puerto Madryn and, lastly, the many people in Wales and Patagonia whose ancestors sailed on *Mimosa,* for whom this book is principally written. *Diolch yn fawr.*

Thanks, too, to various members of my family in Argentina, especially my great-great-aunt, the late Carmen Greene de Lombardini of Vedia in the province of Buenos Aires; and Adela Flaherty de Greene, also of

Vedia, for information on Thomas Greene and his role in the voyage to Patagonia, which led to my deep interest in the ship in which he sailed and in the men, women and children whom he accompanied.

Especially, I would like to thank the wonderful team at Y Lolfa and the Welsh Books Council for their financial support.

Susan Wilkinson
Canada

Prologue

At ten o'clock on the morning of Thursday, May 25, 1865, a twelve-year-old barque, already past her sailing prime, was towed from the vast basin of the Victoria Dock in Liverpool and out into the Mersey, to await her passengers and crew. Her varnish was blistered, her brass-work dull, and her female figurehead had been removed and replaced by a simple scroll, just three days before.

The crew signed on and boarded. They put their gunny sacks or sea-chests containing their clothes and possessions in their allocated places and went about their several tasks. To them, it was a voyage like any other, and the destination made little difference to them. They were informed by the mate, who, with the master, had come aboard the day before, that the ship would be carrying women and children as well as three preachers, and they were warned to mind their manners and language. On that same day, at two o'clock in the afternoon, a young doctor from Ireland, who had completed his medical studies in Edinburgh less than a month before, came aboard as ship's surgeon; and two Welshmen, who had signed on as purser and passenger cook, joined the ship in order to work their passages. The barque remained at anchor in the river for three days, scarcely noticeable among the towering sails and 'moon-rakers' of larger clippers beyond and beside her as rowboats and lighters brought the passengers from Pier Head to board her.

The dilapidated barque – a converted clipper, which had not been designed to carry passengers – was bound for Patagonia, seven-thousand miles away. She had been chartered from her Liverpool owners because the ship originally contracted for the journey – the *Halton Castle* – had been delayed on its return to Liverpool following its voyage around Cape Horn from Valparaiso. More than a hundred and sixty Welsh emigrants boarded the barque, people whose traditions and language were being threatened by the Anglicisation that was engulfing Wales, and whose poverty was driving them to seek a new land.

Save for explorers, naturalists and sealers, few had ever been to Patagonia, and none had stayed. There, free from the oppression of tithes, evictions and poverty, they would be masters of their own destinies, free to make their own laws, speak their own language and follow their own customs and traditions. There, where a land stretched green and splendid to the horizon, they would make a new Wales that would be more Welsh than the old. With the promise of one hundred acres of land for each family, and for each adult male, they had everything to gain and nothing to lose – nothing, that is, except their lives and their illusions.

At four o'clock on Sunday, May 28, the port procedures completed and the winds and tides favourable, a pilot came on board to guide the little clipper towards the open sea, while those on shore stood silent, unwilling to depart while sight of the ship carrying their loved ones to Patagonia remained. Being Sunday, the loading and unloading of ships' cargoes had ceased; and the port, with its miles of docks and warehouses, was silent, its heartbeat temporarily stilled.

As her acres of sails filled out in the wind and she headed into St George's Channel, the Welsh Dragon fluttering from her foremast, none could have known that the little ship was sailing into immortality and that her name would become synonymous with the hopes and dreams, hardships and disillusionments and the eventual triumphs of the passengers she carried.

The name of the ship was *Mimosa*.

Part I

The Building of *Mimosa*

She must be sharp-lined, very long in proportion to beam, (and) built for speed. She must be tall-sparred and carry the utmost spread of canvas.

A B C Whipple, *The Clipper Ships*

Antecedents

The word ship, given to the device by which man contrived to convey himself and his goods upon water, was derived from the old Teutonic word *skap*.

Rafts made of floating logs, bundles of brushwood or reeds, hollowed-out tree trunks, canoes of bark or of skin stretched across a framework of wood, vessels of planks stitched or bound together with leather or fibre cords, even inflated skins of pigs or cows, had been used since time immemorial – and in some parts of the world are still being used – to cross rivers, lakes and even seas. Necessity being the mother of invention, a platform of upright timbers, fenced in and covered over, on sea-going rafts, was found to be effective in keeping the goods and the persons navigating the rafts relatively dry from the wash of the sea. Finally, a *skap* was made by constructing a framework of ribs fastened to a wooden keel, with planking attached by means of wooden pegs, or treenails, to make a hull, a paddle tied to the stern to determine direction, and a square of cloth attached to a pole increased its speed when filled with wind.

Speed and carrying power were increased by the Egyptians, who devised the first known ship, as distinct from a large canoe or raft, in about 3000 BC. By using as many as two dozen rowers on each side of a vessel, they made their explorations along the Nile to the Red Sea and round the coasts of Arabia. A mast made of a thick papyrus root that could support a greater area of sail was adapted to be raised or lowered without the necessity of removing it and laying it flat on the bottom. The bow curved gracefully upwards, like the neck of a backwards-looking swan, and was sometimes ornamented by a figurehead representing a bird, beast or a god; it was removed as the vessel approached shore, so as not to frighten the land spirits. These first known ships were used for war as well as for commerce.

Increased seaworthiness led to increased trade, which, in turn, led to plunder, war and the need for greater speed. The Phoenicians, perhaps the greatest traders of the Ancient World, to whom the development and art of navigation clearly belongs, traversed the length and breadth of the Mediterranean, from Tyre and Sidon, even circumnavigating the coast of Africa, in their long, narrow horse-prowed galleys. They constructed vessels made from the cedars of Lebanon, capable of carrying ever larger cargoes, and established trading posts like Gadés which, in time, grew into independent settlements like Cadiz. Phoenicia was conquered by the inland Assyrians, who sailed up and down the Tigris and Euphrates in their biremes, which were copied from the Phoenician galleys.

As commerce flourished, the Cushites and the Libyans constructed towers along the Mediterranean coast, and priests maintained beacon fires in them to warn of rocks or other hidden dangers. A lighthouse, called the Pharos of Alexandria, which stood some two hundred feet tall and was crowned by a lantern and a statue of Poseidon, was one of the seven wonders of the Ancient World. Rhodes grew in importance; and a code of maritime laws, such as the division of ship ownership into sixty-four equal shares, was drawn up by Rhodian sea traders and passed into universal usage.

Speed was further increased by the biremes of the Greek city states, manned by crews which, in true democratic fashion, shared the labour of rowing, irrespective of rank or birth. From the bireme came the trireme, developed in Corinth. A bow, fashioned into an imaginary sea monster and covered with bronze, formed a ram. The trireme was the warship of Athens during her prime. It was superseded by the development of the quadrireme, quinquereme, and on to the vessels of sixteen tiers of oars, which necessitated an elaborate system of seating and positioning to keep the rowers synchronized.

The Romans were deficient in naval construction, until a Carthaginian quinquereme drifted ashore and gave them a model for future fleets, which they powered by enslaved rowers chained to their benches. The old ramming tactics of the Greek city states gave way to sickle-headed spars that mowed through the rigging of enemy ships. Rome added little to the feats of exploration, concentrating more on development of battle.

With eventual stability in the Mediterranean came an increase in trade, necessitating the building of a different kind of vessel. These, like the great Egyptian corn ships, which brought supplies from Alexandria to the Italian ports, or the vessels transporting stone and marble for the glorification of Rome or Venice, were propelled, not by banks of oars, but by sails, and the steering side-paddle was replaced by a fixed rudder as a means of directing a ship's course. The seafaring republics of Venice and Genoa rose and prospered, far surpassing nations like Britain, struggling for maritime supremacy, where the size or measurement of ships was assessed on the basis of how many tuns or casks of wine they could carry. The Frankish and Viking powers, in their tall-prowed ships, born to the use of oar and sail, menaced the northern seas as far as Iceland and Greenland, and devised a method for increasing or decreasing the spread of canvas by reefing.

Until the 15th century, ships carried one mast, with one enormous square sail attached to a horizontal yard that could be raised, lowered and even swivelled around. When not in use, it was tied around a long pole, called a bowsprit, extending forwards from the prow. Structures, called castles, rising above the stem and stern, that came to be known as fore-castles and aft-castles, defined defensive or offensive positions in naval battles.

The Crusaders set out for the Holy Land in single-masted, square-rigged vessels chartered from the Portuguese, Pisans and Genoese, whose captains observed from their protective fore-castles and aft-castles that the Turks and the Saracens built the hulls of their caravels with planking fitted edge to edge, and compared them to their own heavier, clinker-built hulls with overlapping edges. Horizons and spheres of knowledge widened. An appetite for the silks and spices of the East and for exploration of lands beyond their own horizons was whetted and instilled.

The Portuguese and Spanish sailed west across the Atlantic in smooth-hulled vessels they now called *caravelas,* which had a second or mizzen mast to carry a second sail. In the middle of the century, ships were needed to transport to Portugal African slaves captured by the Moors – a trade which considerably enriched the Portuguese seaports, much as it was to enrich Liverpool and Bristol in later centuries. Pilgrims, too, required transport to the shrines of St James of Compostela in Northern Spain and Saint Thomas Becket at Canterbury as well as to the Holy Land. To calculate a ship's speed, a weighted piece of wood with a line tied to it – the log – was tossed over the stern. The length of line let out in an hour was measured by a knot tied in the line. Nautical miles were measured in *knots*, and were recorded in a *log* book. A third mast, the foremast, that carried the foresail, was developed to aid steering.

In the 16th century, the English, too, began their navigations and search for passages around or through inconveniently placed continents; these would culminate in an empire that covered three quarters of the known world. They sailed in galleons whose hulls, broad at the waterline and tapering inwards along their lengths, provided a greater cargo-carrying capacity in their holds, as well as space for ever-heavier cannon along their sides. Galleries in the form of open-air balconies went around the stern portion, while innovations in rigging enabled portions of sail to be taken down or be raised up, according to weather conditions.

Venice, in her wily dotage, no longer dominated the European trade in spices and silks, as younger Atlantic nations flexed their maritime muscles. During the 17th and 18th centuries, the expansion of trade and mercantile enterprises was incessant, as the light caravels of the 15th and 16th centuries gave way to stately two- and three-decked ships propelled by sail, armed with cannon, and broad in the beam. Commercial rivalry inevitably led to conflict and frequently to war. Antwerp, where over two thousand ships docked daily, passed the zenith of its power as the general storehouse and emporium of the world, a distinction that was envied by Britain.

The risks of trade and commerce grew too considerable to be borne by single individuals, and companies like the Hanseatic League, Company of Russian Merchants, and the British East India Company came into being. Shippers became involved with claims for exclusive rights in trading, waging war, captures and burnings, confiscations and fierce reprisals. Vessels were armed for aggression and defence, and, for safety and attack, travelled in fleets. The East India Company built its fleet of sturdy East Indiamen, designed to perform the functions of merchant vessels, passenger ships and, when required to do so, men-of-war, and fought its way through Portuguese obstructions to the Indian coast, while the Dutch, the French and the Swedes formed similar companies to compete with trade of the East and West. To protect British shipping and in an effort to check the increasing power of the Dutch, Cromwell's parliament decreed that only British ships could transport goods into British ports.

The seas swarmed with privateers, many of them American or French, and, wherever trade existed, smuggling became endemic. Ships, whether frigates for war or merchantmen, required large crews, comprising men who were often pressed or crimped. In London, a group of merchants with interests in shipping began to meet in a coffee house in Lombard Street; it was owned by one Edward Lloyd and became known familiarly as Lloyd's. Its customers were able to read the current shipping news, which Lloyd published as a weekly broadsheet.

At the beginning of the 19th century, a new kind of ship was about to evolve. It was called a clipper. It came from America, and it was the fastest sailing ship that the world had ever known.

The Clipper

Three things defined a clipper: sharp lines, speed and great sail-carrying capability. There were 'clippers', 'medium clippers' and 'extreme clippers', depending on the degree of sharpness of the hull. The term 'China clippers' appeared in the mid 1860s, at the height of the China tea trade, while the term 'tea clipper' appeared only when such vessels had all but ceased to exist.

The first clipper, built in Baltimore, twenty-one years before *Mimosa*'s construction, did not suddenly appear in all its racing glory; it evolved from innovations to the schooner, and because the times and the need for faster ships were right for it.

Protected by Cromwell's Navigation Laws, limiting imports to

Britain to being carried only by British ships, and with the powerful East India Company having the monopoly of trade of all islands, ports, havens, creeks and cities of Asia, Africa and America, there had been no foreign competition before the middle decades of the 19th century. The East India Company, which virtually created British India and founded Hong Kong, was the single most powerful economic force that the world had ever known. It had its own armies, palaces, courts, currencies and territories; and the lavishness of its hospitality in entertaining foreign dignitaries was legendary. The thick-sided, flat-bottomed, apple-cheek-bowed East Indiamen that sat plump and comfortable in the water had, as well, the monopoly of the lucrative tea trade. Comfort and safety were valued over speed; and the one-way voyage from China to England could take as much as two years – a one-year sailing to China was an unusually fast voyage. The East Indiamen, or 'tea-wagons', as they were derisively nicknamed, sailed slowly and never at night, taking down their sails and anchoring at sunset, even in the calmest of seas, so that the teas they carried inevitably lost their freshness and much of their value by the time they had been unloaded in the East or West India Docks in London. With the repeal of Cromwell's Navigation Laws and the end to the East India Company's monopoly, ships of any nationality could carry tea from China to England and snatch that lucrative market for themselves.

Other horizons of trade opened, particularly in South America. In December 1850, a 1003-ton American clipper named *Oriental* sailed up the Thames and docked at the West India Docks with a cargo of tea; she was the first ship to carry tea to England since the repeal of the Navigation Laws. She caused a sensation, since she had taken only ninety-one days to sail from Hong Kong against the monsoon; with the monsoon winds in her favour, she would have made it in less time. No one had ever seen such a large and speedy clipper before, and British shipbuilders were not slow in copying details of her slender lines into their sketch books, as they estimated with shrewd eyes the length of her three masts and the expanse of her sail plan. Faster sailing ships were now needed for faster voyages, and, to the humiliation of British shipbuilders, the fastest ships were American.

Some years before, in Aberdeen, a young ship designer had been commissioned to build a small schooner for local coastal trade. By experimentation, he devised an entirely new hull shape, drastically altering the shape of the bow to make it long and narrow, rising in a smooth curve, so that it formed a cutwater. The Aberdeen bow, as it came to be called, became the trademark of the world's fastest sailing ships called clippers.

The name of the designer was William Hall.

The Shipyard

Mimosa's life began in Scotland, some three years after the sensational arrival of the *Oriental* in the Thames, as a sketch by her designer, William Hall of Alexander Hall & Sons, the leading shipbuilders in Aberdeen. Robert Vining and William Killey, Liverpool merchants and co-partners in trading, had placed an order for a medium-sized clipper of 500 tons or less to add to the other clippers Robert Vining had commissioned from them.

Alexander Hall & Sons had revolutionized merchant shipping the world over with the design of the Aberdeen bow, in 1839. As well as its length, a vessel was measured for depth and breadth, at three different parts of the hull: stern, bow and amidships. By extending the stem forward to a raked angle and by cutting away the stern to make it overhang, there was some extra cargo space in the front and back of the hull, and volume measurements could not be made on curves. Not every ship owner was enamoured of so revolutionary a design, and, at first, there was some opposition to it. When it was seen, though, that the ships with the Halls' Aberdeen bow, as well as attaining greater speeds, were capable of carrying more cargo than was required to be registered, resulting in larger profits for the owners, interest became universally keen, taxes and harbour dues being assessed on the approximate weight of cargo registered.

William Hall had already built two ships for Robert Vining. Five years before, in 1848, Alexander Hall & Sons had built the 328-ton clipper, *Reindeer*, for Robert Vining and his then partner in trading, Thomas McTear. This vessel had broken all records in speed on the China tea run and had been the first to arrive in London with the new season's teas. Under her master, the renowned Austrian-born Antony Enwright, *Reindeer* arrived in the Thames only two days behind the famed and far larger *Oriental*, with tea loaded in Whampoa. In the same year as *Reindeer* was launched, 1848, the shipyard launched *Bonita*, a small clipper of 299 tons, also for Thomas McTear and Robert Vining. *Mimosa* was the first ship to be built for Robert Vining's new partnership with William Killey, a former master mariner, who had owned shares in *Bonita*.

The new clipper, to be called *Mimosa*, was to be designed for the South American trade as well as for the China tea trade. The only stipulation demanded by her Liverpool owners was that she be medium-sized so that a full cargo could, as far as possible, be guaranteed on every voyage, and that she be fast. As well as the profits being accrued from the growing South American trade, fortunes were being amassed on the China to England tea runs, for all Europe except for Russia got the bulk of their tea through Britain; and the shipyard had numerous orders for clippers suitable for the triangular trade route to Australia with mining or agricultural equipment, across to China with coal, and home to London with tea. When the monopoly of the East India Company was abolished in 1832 (twenty years before *Mimosa* was built), and with it the duties and taxes levied by them, an era of rapid expansion of tea importation from China began; and so did the era of building fast ships to transport it from the Chinese ports to London, the warehouse and central tea market for the world.

From the beginning, speed was of primary importance. Smuggling, piracy, snatching trade from prohibited ports, even slave and opium running demanded speed in ships. Although trade grew more respectable, and even legal, speed still counted. As trade around the world increased, so did the need for ships to carry tea from China, baled wool from Australia, tools, provisions and liquor for the gold rush in California, cotton, sugar and guano from South America, and carry them fast.

William Hall knew the necessity for speed. Was not the very word 'clipper' derived from 'clip', as in 'to go at a fair clip'? In the volatile world of trade, where fortunes were as mercurial as the rising or plummeting commodity prices on which such fortunes depended, speed of delivery was essential, especially for so perishable a commodity as tea. No longer was a leisurely two-year passage out and back the norm. The new clipper must be fast enough to make the fifteen-thousand-mile journey from Shanghai or Foochong to London in little more than a hundred days, and be strong enough to withstand the monsoons that buffeted the China seas in summer and winter. Since she must be fast enough to out-sail the clippers of rival merchants, strength and cargo-carrying capacity would be forfeited for speed.

She was not intended for the China tea trade alone, but for the South American trade to the Brazils, where Vining & Killey had commercial interests. *Mimosa* would not be sturdy enough to combat the murderous gales and mountain-high seas of Cape Horn, but would be built for the more moderate winds of the Indian and Atlantic Oceans; and her sail plan would enable her to ghost in light airs, which would becalm a 2000-ton Yankee clipper. Speed, however, depended also on factors such as the direction and intensity of the wind, or lack of wind, so that it was impossible to guarantee a definite speed for a given voyage. Stability, too, depended principally on the amount of ballast carried, and the correct amount was determined experimentally, after completion of the vessel. William Hall could design her to be fast, but he could not guarantee *how* fast. In the end, her speed, stability and performance would depend upon how her various masters would drive her and how she would respond to the hand at her helm.

Throughout the 1840s shipbuilding was in the doldrums. In 1848, five years before *Mimosa*'s construction, only three clippers were built in all the shipyards in Aberdeen, one of these being Robert Vining's *Reindeer*, which immediately gained distinction for making the best runs of any clipper in the China tea trade. In 1849, the year that Alexander Hall died, the Cromwellian Navigation Laws were repealed, despite predictably violent opposition. The carrying trade of Britain and her colonies was thrown open to all nations, and competition, especially from America, increased. With the abolition of navigational restrictions, orders for new clippers to compete with Yankee clippers poured in, and shipyards everywhere were building clippers as fast as they could. New markets opened and freight prices increased, with the result that merchants could not find sufficient capacity to fulfil their orders to carry cargoes to and from all parts of the world. Aberdeen became the primary shipbuilding centre in Britain. As yet, not one shipyard in the rest of Britain could compete with those of Aberdeen – and Alexander Hall & Sons owned its leading shipyard. In 1853, when *Mimosa* was being built, William Hall was aged forty-seven and responsible for design, while his brother James, a year younger, was the shipyard manager

Every clipper was designed to be an improvement on her predecessor, and *Mimosa*'s predecessors performed well. Among them were *Scottish*

Maid, the first vessel with William Hall's Aberdeen bow, *Glentanar, William Punton, Lightning, Acasta,* and *Torrington,* which was built specifically for the opium trade for the renowned mercantile house of Jardine Matheson & Co. and was the very first British clipper in the China seas. There were also *Bon Accord, Electra, North Star, Bonita, Reindeer, Benjamin Elkin, Pilot Fish, Stornoway, John Taylor, Chrysolite, Hannibal, Julia, Cairngorm,* and *Leichardt.* Perhaps *Mimosa* would be William Hall's masterpiece and receive mention in the *Illustrated London News,* as had his splendid *Cairngorm* and some of his other ships. He would have liked *carte blanche,* so that *Mimosa's* speed and finish would not be surpassed by any vessel afloat, that she would be the best vessel of her class and tonnage; but he did not have that freedom of design. Owners' instructions always impeded his ambition to design the perfect clipper. Besides, it was an expensive gamble, to build a ship like his near-perfect *Cairngorm* on speculation, built earlier that year, although, with the shipyard's reputation, he had had no trouble in finding a buyer from one of the large mercantile tea companies; and *Cairngorm* sailed under the flag of Jardine Matheson & Co. With the restrictions imposed upon him, *Mimosa* would not be a perfect clipper, but she would be good enough for what Robert Vining and William Killey required of her, which was to get a good return on their investment.

Since she was intended to be a merchant ship, she would carry no passengers, but William Hall knew that sometimes the owners or their relatives liked to travel in their ships, so he decided to provide for a spare cabin in the poop accommodation.

In his zeal to design a clipper that would be a refinement on her predecessors, William Hall drew up plans for a three-masted ship; the length to breadth ratio of the hull would be no more than 4 to 1; and he calculated the loftiest masts and the widest sails that she could bear for her size.

She would go at a fair clip, all right.

Alexander Hall & Sons

As William Hall sat in his office, making some elementary sketches for Robert Vining's new clipper and scribbling calculations of possible mast heights and hull dimensions on a sheet of paper, he felt on top of the world. Due to his invention of the Aberdeen bow, the shipyard could barely keep up with orders for clippers. He had another cause for happiness: his wife, Catherine, had informed him that she was expecting another child. He hoped it would be a daughter this time, a sister for young William, Alexander and wee James. With another baby on the way, a new clipper to design and a full order book, he had every reason to be happy.

It is easy to imagine what it was like there, at the time. In the yard below, eight-year-old William was 'helping' one of the carpenters, and William Hall smiled at the sound of his son's chatter, and watched as he struggled to drag a wooden treenail as long as his arm towards the whale-like curved ribs that were being hammered into place on the blocks. Catherine was continually anxious for the safety of the two older boys in the shipyard, worried lest they fall under one of the huge timbers.

William smiled at Alexander, whose dark head was bent over a sheet of paper, absorbed in his drawing of a ship. At five, Alexander could draw a ship with the correct amount of sails and a recognizable hull. When he grew up, Alexander would become a designer of ships, like his father and his great-grandfather, James Cochar, William Hall thought with pride. It was in his blood. The shipyard, founded by his grandfather, Alexander Hall, after whom the boy was named, would continue to prosper under young Alexander and his brothers. He was sure of that.

★

Alexander Hall was born in 1760, the son of a crofter, also called Alexander Hall, of Kirkton of Auchterless in Aberdeenshire. As soon as he could walk, he helped with tasks on the small croft his father leased. Rent was paid partly in money, some in oats and the poultry his mother raised, and the rest in labour, to which he was soon contributing, by cutting peat, or loading coal or shell lime from the seaports of Banff or Macduff, some twenty miles to the north, and delivering it to the laird's estate. In the whole of the decreasing parish of Auchterless, of which Kirkton was just one of the small, widespread crofter communities, there were no hills to provide stone for building, and fences were made by planting thorn hedges.

Although Alexander Hall's father had been born in Auchterless, his grandfather's family had originally come from Otterburn in Northumberland, in the lea of the Cheviot Hills, where they owned considerably more land and prestige than Alexander Hall's father did in wind-lashed fields of Auchterless. Alexander Hall's grandfather, John Hall, had been forced to leave Northumberland after his father, also called John, had been tried and executed in London for his part in the abortive Jacobite rising of 1715. Driven out of Northumberland and forced into hiding when the family estates were sequestered and held forfeit to the Crown, young John Hall fled to Scotland with little other than the family Bible, a little money, the clothes he wore on his back, and a burning hatred of the English.

As Alexander Hall grew to boyhood, he showed little inclination to follow in his father's footsteps. Not for him, he quickly decided, would be the back-breaking drudge of clearing a patch of ground of gorse and heather for a bare subsistence of oats and turnips or, if he were lucky, a small flock of sheep. He would not become enslaved to a few acres of land that gave so grudgingly of its bounty, or to the shadow of rising rents and eviction by a laird who deemed it more profitable to clear his land of crofters at the end of their leases. He would not marry, only to have his wife grow prematurely old from work and worry like his mother, whose fingers were bent and arthritic from knitting stockings for the factories in

Aberdeen, so that he could have shoes to wear on Sundays and books for the small school she insisted he attend.

It was wood, he discovered, with which he loved to work. He loved the smell of a healthy pine, the roughness of its bark, its gummy residue. He loved the smell of the oaks that were sometimes felled around the laird's estate, with their concentric circles denoting their age. He loved the feel of the outer bark that could be rendered silk-smooth with proper use of a plane. Nothing ugly could ever be made from wood. It could not be twisted into sharp, contorted shapes, unlike iron. Like a creature of flesh and blood, wood had a natural life span.

When he was twenty-three, young Alexander Hall went to Aberdeen, travelling the fifty miles eastwards by cart and on foot, along drovers' paths and coach roads, to see if he could find work as a ships' carpenter and, if possible, to learn the art of ship drafting. Chance directed his steps to Footdee, a small fishing village comprising half a dozen rows of low, thatched cottages and high sand dunes on a little toe of land where the River Dee empties its clear waters into the greyness of the North Sea. Here, two small shipyards made Aberdeen's 20- to 80-ton fishing vessels, sloops and schooners. Fate directed him to the shipyard of Alexander Gibbon and James Cochar, on the Pocra Pier, where he was taken on as a ships' carpenter and apprentice draftsman.

Footdee had been a shipping port and a fishing village since the Middle Ages, and its geographical location on the North Sea coast guaranteed an abundant trade in herring. It had existed since the 13th century as a cluster of houses on the northeast shore of the estuary of the Dee, and had been known as Foty, or Fittie, either named after St Fotyn or after the marshy land, or *feithe*, that surrounded the area. The harbour was bank-full of water at high tide, and a hollow of sandbanks and pools when the tide was out. Because of the silt washed down by the Dee and the extremes of the tides, only small vessels could come in as far as Footdee, which limited the size of ships built there. The fishing vessels were frequently made by the fishermen themselves, and were dragged across the narrow isthmus of land to the estuary. So inadequate was the harbour that, in 1676, Aberdeen having a total of nine vessels, Pocra Pier was built and the water surrounding it deepened. From that time on, shipping in Footdee slowly began to prosper.

Alexander Hall had chosen well by going to Gibbon & Cochar. Alexander Gibbon came from a long line of shipwrights, and James Cochar, whose own father had been a shipbuilder in Montrose, was a draftsman of vision, who foresaw that the age of building ships by eye must give way to mathematical formulae and scientific design. One of the first shipbuilders of the more modern age, if not *the* first, James Cochar's skill in mathematics was destined to take ship design to new heights; it was so innovative that he kept his formulae a closely-guarded secret. In the seven years of Alexander Hall's apprenticeship, James Cochar taught him everything he knew about ship design and shipbuilding, binding him neither to divulge the knowledge nor to apprentice himself to any other shipbuilder.

James Cochar was a relentless taskmaster. Under his strict supervision, Alexander Hall learned that the exterior parts of a ship, the bottom and sides, were spoken of as the shell, which, in combination with the decks, supplied the strength required for the structure as a whole. He learned that the frames of the shell running across the ship, like the rafters in the roof of his father's croft or the ribs in his own body, were called transverse frames or ribs, and that those that ran under the deck were called beams. He learned that the parts of the frames at the bottom of the ship had to be made deep and strong, in order to support the ship when she was docked or grounded, and were known as floors, while the spaces between the floors are spoken of as the bilges, and that they were held upright in their proper positions by other frames, called keelsons. He learned, too, about other supports needed to enable a vessel to withstand heavy seas in bad weather, about partitions in the internal spaces of the ship, called bulkheads, about knees and vertical pillars needed to support the decks and the bulkheads. He learned about yards and sheets, about clew lines, buntlines and ratlines, and the acres of sail needed to propel a ship across the oceans of the world.

James Cochar insisted, too, that his young protégé attend with his own family the little stone kirk, where the sounds of waves pounding on the shore and the ceaseless wash of pebbles accompanied the voices raised in song and praise. Alexander Hall willingly complied with both conditions, and, when he was thirty years old, he was made a partner in the firm. He also asked for and was granted the hand in marriage of James Cochar's daughter, Elizabeth, who was sixteen years his junior.

In 1793, when Alexander Hall was thirty-three, James Cochar died. For a while Alexander Hall joined another shipbuilder; but the partnership of Buchan & Hall was not long-lasting. Gibbon also died; and Hall & Co. Carpenters came into being.

Even the four shipyards of Gill, Brebner & Stephen, William Rennie, Nichol & Reed, and Hall & Co. that were now established in Footdee could not keep pace with the orders for ships and schooners. The only land communication was by stage coach or cart, so that the exports and imports of Aberdeen were practically all sea-borne. Alexander Hall's star was clearly on the rise.

Footdee, known in Latin charters as Vicus de Fotin, suited him well. With just over two hundred souls, it seemed like a metropolis in comparison to Auchterless. It was a close-knit community, so isolated from the main town of Aberdeen that few had ever been there. Fittie men were rough and dour, and he liked their independence. In times of war against England in centuries past, Fittie men had laid their fishing boats end to end across the mouth of the Dee, to form a pontoon bridge for the kilted warriors of Aberdeen to cross; and when, in later centuries, they were rebuked for holding a fish market in Aberdeen on the Sabbath, they continued to wheel their carts of herring across the sandy isthmus at low tide, despite the censure of church bells.

They were superstitious, too: water kelpies, ghosts and mermaids were as real to them as the vicious cold of the North Sea gales. Every fisherman, as he crossed the threshold of his cottage, had salt sprinkled on him by his wife for good luck and a safe return. To mention a man of the cloth while at sea was deemed to court certain disaster. So-called unlucky men were forbidden to undo the moorings of a boat that was setting out for the fishing grounds.

Life was hard in Footdee. The men, when not employed in one of the four shipyards, lived by fishing; the women contributed by gutting herring in sheds that were ice cold, winter and summer, or by gathering seaweed from the shore; the children helped by baiting miles of lines with shelled mussels. The fishing families lived in low, dank cottages on the quayside; their windows were ever salted by the spray of the North Sea. Few had the luxury of a dividing wall. For most, a sail cloth attached to either wall provided the only semblance of privacy. Ceilings were formed by old oars that supported driftwood. The front of each line of cottages looked onto the back of the next and onto the dunghills crossed by spars, on which hung lines of drying skate and the skins of dogs, blown out of their natural shapes and tarred, for use as fishing net buoys. There was one source of water, from a spring-fed well in the centre of the village that was worked by a pump; and oil from fish livers provided Footdee's only lighting. Wrecks and storms were frequent. The sea gave and took away in equal measure, and Alexander Hall became acquainted with the joy of bountiful catches and the grief when men who fished too long in rising seas failed to return.

Over the years, he saw Footdee grow. The Road to Pocra (a derivation from *pock* and *raw*, meaning a street of baskets) became York Street. The sand dunes were levelled, the land reclaimed. The harbour was further improved, so that boats no longer had to be dragged across the strip of land that separated the shipyards from the beach in order to be launched. The thatched hovels with their dunghills of human ordure were torn down; in their place six neat rows of slate-roofed cottages were built, in two quadrangles, named North Square and South Square. Houses were built for the pilots who were increasingly needed to guide boats into deep water or into the shallower depths of the harbour to berth.

Alexander Hall and his wife, Elizabeth, had thirteen children – five sons and eight daughters – of whom all but six died in infancy or childhood. They lived in one of the four slate-roofed houses near the brickworks on the Pocra Road, later named York Street. Two enormous whale ribs formed an arch at the little gate that overlooked the sea. His children attended the only school in Footdee, located near the shipyard, where they learned to read and write and studied the elements of navigation, under a schoolmaster to whom the sea was as much a part of life as it was for his pupils. Alexander Hall knew the fishermen of Footdee, and his sons and daughters knew the children for whom shelling a thousand mussels before, or even instead of, school was a daily routine. He was respected and liked by the men he employed. He attended their weddings in the kirk where he himself had been married, danced with the bride

Alexander Hall & Sons shipyard staff, 1862. Standing, from left to right: Alex. H Wilson, shipbuilder, J M Carnie, foreman carpenter, Wm. Ligertwood, boat builder, Alex. Guyan, gatekeeper, George Sim, carpenter, John Hadden, block-maker, James Morrison, blacksmith, Wm. Shearer, cashier, John Gunn, foreman carpenter, Peter Anderson, foreman joiner, WILLIAM HALL, ALEX. HALL Jnr., JAMES HALL, Wm. Goodbrand, carpenter. Seated, left to right: James Shand, foreman carpenter, Walter Dinnet, foreman carpenter, Robt. Robertson, blacksmith, James Mitchell, foreman carpenter, James Anderson Jnr., carpenter, John Cruickshank, office boy, Robert Croll, office boy.

while the fiddlers played through the night; and the Carpenters' Ball, held every Hogmanay in the shipyard mould loft, was Footdee's social event of the year.

When William and James, his only sons who were to survive him, were aged five and four, Alexander Hall launched his first ship. Others followed in quick succession: steam packets, whale-boats, schooners, and he employed a bookkeeper to keep an account of the ships he built. His 582-ton vessel, *Asia,* built for the East Indian trade when William and James were thirteen and fourteen respectively, created a sensation; it was the largest ship ever built in Aberdeen. Every man, woman and child of Footdee as well as crowds from Scotland and England came to see her launched, a military band playing on her deck.

John Duthie, one of Alexander Hall's former foremen, began his own shipyard, and when he built his first ship, Alexander Hall was the first to congratulate him. The shipyard of Gill, Brebner & Stephen had long gone; and William Stephen's grandsons were beginning to build ships in their own yards in Glasgow and Dundee. Another rival, William Rennie, had left Aberdeen for Nova Scotia, from where he would eventually return to build his own line of China clippers in Liverpool. Messrs. John Vernon came and went; and when they went, Walter Hood took over their yard; he was to become famed all over the world for his line of fast-sailing clippers. His *Thermopylae,* which rivalled the *Cutty Sark,* was from the design of one of Alexander Hall's former apprentices. In time, Alexander Hall's shipyard would absorb that of Walter Hood. By then, it would cover four acres of the eleven acres comprising Footdee.

When Alexander Hall retired in 1835, aged seventy-five, leaving his sons to run the shipyard, Alexander Hall & Sons was the foremost shipyard, not only in Aberdeen, but in the whole of Britain. He died in 1849, when he was eighty-nine.[1]

Process of Design

When a shipbuilder was invited to construct a ship, he was informed of the trade for which the vessel was intended, the desired speed, the weight of her cargo, the number of her passengers, if any, likely to be carried, and the length and duration of her intended voyages. These requirements imposed certain limits on size, cost and tonnage, which could not be exceeded. Her desired classification was to be stated, as this determined the kind and quality of wood to be used in her construction. (Since *Mimosa* was to have the highest classification, defined by *Lloyd's* as A1, her frame would be built of oak, with three layers of larch.) Sometimes the details of a similar ship were used as a benchmark, against which refinements and modifications could be made. Building a clipper involved a measure of intuition, since no two clipper hulls were exactly alike. Each was unique, in an attempt to create the perfect sailing ship that would be an improvement on its predecessor.

Outline drawings were first prepared, to take account of the dimensions required, and calculations were made of the size and weight of the hull, length of masts and number of sails the ship could reasonably bear. Next, the final calculations of trim, stability and speed were made.

Drawings were made of the deck and sail plan, the holds and spaces for cargo, and passenger and crew accommodation. A specification was drawn up of all particulars of the vessel, including details as to the quality of the materials to be used and how and from where those parts not manufactured by the shipbuilder, such as pumps, rigging and anchors, were to be obtained.

The design drawings completed, a half-model of *Mimosa*'s hull was constructed and sent to Robert Vining and William Killey for their approval. Like a pull-apart toy, the interconnecting sections of pine or mahogany, planed and chiselled to perfection, formed in miniature

Mimosa's hull. The other side, being a mirror image of the half-model, needed no sculpting. On the half-model, William Hall carefully drew *Mimosa's* main frames, together with the positions of her decks and hatchways.

With the half-model duly approved by her future owners in Liverpool, the lines of her hull were chalked to full size on the smoothly-planed and blackened mould loft floor, to serve as templates for the preparation of *Mimosa's* ribs.

Because they were so hard-driven and suffered so much wear and

Mould loft (note buckets to put out fires).

tear, a clipper's seagoing life rarely exceeded a decade. Fully a quarter came to grief before they were ten years old, pounded to pieces on reefs or lost in storms. Even as he received the approval from Robert Vining and William Killey to proceed with the construction, William Hall must have experienced sadness in knowing that, by the law of averages, the little clipper was destined for a short life. He only hoped that it would be a memorable one.

The Timber

The prime requisites in good hull timber were strength and durability. The range of woods was, however, restricted to a few. Fir was not durable and splintered too easily. Elm and beech could, if necessary, be used for keels. Teak or mahogany were normally used for the deckhouse and trims.

Oak was the best hull timber, and even that varied in suitability, depending upon its species. Baltic oak could be used for planking, but not for the hull. Italian oak was so hard that the tools working it frequently broke, and the planks could not easily be curved. American white oak was susceptible to dry rot. English oak was conceded to be the best shipbuilding wood, for its hardness and durability. If, however, the tree was too young, the proportion of sap was too great; if it was too old, its timber was brittle and predisposed to early decay. The ideal age for an oak to be cut was when it was a hundred years old.

Since time immemorial, the oak tree was sacred. Worship of the oak was widely practised by Greeks, Romans, Norsemen, the ancient Germans, and the Slavs, who associated it with Jupiter, Zeus, Thor, Thunar or Perun, and by the Celts and Druids, for whom nothing was more sacred than the mistletoe and the oak on which it grew. Religious rites were enacted in its groves. Sacrifices of heifers, rams or cocks were made to it for bountiful crops or rain. Only the wood of the oak was used to kindle the sacred Beltane fires. Its mistletoe was held to possess curative and magic powers, which, to be effective, should be gathered at certain seasons and phases of the moon. In parts of Dalmatia and the lands along the Danube, oaks were believed to have been inhabited by spirits, or even by souls, and that to cut them induced suffering and pain in the tree. Woodcutters felling a healthy oak would first apologize to it, in order not to arouse the hatred of the oak-spirit believed to dwell within, and then would do their task with as tender a regard as if performing an amputation on a human limb.

The time for cutting the timber was imbued with myth, superstition and tradition. Hesiod, considered to be a contemporary of Homer, in his poem on agriculture, *The Works and the Days*, wrote that the cold season was best for cutting ship timber. The Roman architect, Vitruvius, advocated cutting trees to the pith, to allow escape of the rot-inducing sap, and that felling should take place only from early autumn until the end of winter. The Italian architect, Bartolomeo Crescentio, averred that some galleys bought by Pope Sixtus V were rotten within five years because the known customs of cutting timber had been disregarded. King Alfonso the Wise of Spain advocated that timber for ships should be cut 'in the right time'. In France, Napoleon decreed that the felling of naval timber should take place only from November to March, and on the wane of the moon. In 1766, also in France, the master shipbuilder, Duhamel du Monceau, attempted to confute the superstition that the moon affected the timber, and had a number of trees cut at different lunar phases. In 1800, the British Admiralty, in their methodical way, made their own investigations and had a ship built one half of timber cut in spring and the other half of timber cut in winter. When the ship was demolished three years later, there was no difference to be found; all the timber was in the same stage of rot. Despite the Admiralty's findings, in Britain, it was widely held, even until the latter part of the 19th century, that the full moon was the best time for cutting ship timber and that the wind should blow from the north.

It is unlikely that the timber for *Mimosa* was felled in moonlight; but, as in all superstitions, there was a scientific basis for the selection of the season for cutting oak. In spring or autumn, the sap, which was the primary cause of early decay in wood, was rising. Therefore, the most favourable months for cutting were from November to the first half of March. It was thought, too, that girdling, or stripping the bark from a living tree, condensed the sap and made the wood harder and stronger. Girdling, or barking, was executed in the spring before the winter when the selected tree was to be cut, when the sap was rising. Girdling of trees intended for shipbuilding was in vogue in France as early as 1439; in the 18th century, all ships built in Russia were constructed from girdled timber; and, in 1863, ten years after *Mimosa* was built, when the age of iron-built ships had evolved, girdling still had its enthusiasts.

Glen Tanar

The forest of Glen Tanar, in Aboyne, Aberdeenshire, supplied the Hall shipyard with timber for all their ships, *Mimosa* included.

Glen Tanar is a glen of rugged beauty, situated some thirty-odd miles from Aberdeen. It is bound on the north by the River Dee and on the west, south and east by the Grampian Mountains. Old moss roads, where herders drove their long-horned highland cattle, black-faced sheep and their goats, wound amongst ancient oaks, pines, beech, larch and alder. The pines, unlike the larch that were introduced centuries before from Russia, constituted part of the ancient Caledonian forest, which, before the Ice Age, covered the whole of Scotland. The glen was criss-crossed with sheep runs and deer tracks, and wild pigs rooted and foraged for acorns. Deep in the hearts of its hills, topazes and quartz crystals of pale rose are embedded in the granite. Purple and white valerian grows along crumbling stone walls, and the blue of the gentian and wild iris rivals the sky.

Several steep tracks lead over the mountains of Glen Tanar. One, passing through the highest point of the glen, is the Fir Mounth road, along which, it is reputed, Macbeth fled from his castle in Dunsinane to his death at the hand of Malcolm Canmore at Lumphanan, less than five miles from Aboyne. Etnach is a deviant of the Gaelic *aitionnach*, from *aitionn*, a juniper, signifying 'a place of junipers', is a heather-clad moor near the head of the glen. The crystal-clear Water of the Tanar, along which crowfoot and celandine bestow their gold, rises in Mount Keen, one of the most beautiful mountains in Scotland, which towers over the glen to a height of over three thousand feet. (Tanar is derived from an Indo-European root *ta*, 'to flow', and is part of the pre-Celtic group of names of which, in Britain, the 'Thames' is the main representative.) It is joined by the Water of the Gairney and the Water of the Allachy, which together leap and cascade with great swiftness, to enter the Dee a mile above Aboyne.

A holy hermit, one Lesmo, was reputed to have lived in Glen Tanar, finding his heaven in the thick canopy of leaves above him that turned russet from green every season, and his hell in the heavy snows of winter and the gales that levelled trees and swept away bridges when the river was in flood. He died in 731. Fallen circles of lichen-covered stones bear witness to the presence of Celt, Roman and Dane, whose spirits, perhaps, inhabited the ancient oaks and whispered among the pines that were young when they were old. Dispersed Knights of the Templar found sanctuary in the glen's vicinity, in *Tiran Teampull*, before their order vanished forever. The first battle of the Civil War was fought on the Dee. Following the execution of Charles I, Glen Tanar was scoured for

Royalist sympathisers by Cromwell's grim-faced soldiers garrisoned in Aboyne. Then, there followed the Jacobite rebellion in 1745. Under the guise of a deer hunt in Glen Tanar, the kilted clan chiefs, with their packs of hunting dogs and their followers, swore their allegiance to a bonny prince who was one of their own; and when they took refuge in the forest, following the slaughter at Culloden, the Water of the Tanar ran red with their blood.

The union of the parishes of Aboyne – the historic seat of the Earls of Aboyne – and the poorer parish of Glen Tanar took place in the second half of the 17th century. A mile east of where the Dee, confined to a channel, sluices swiftly over a ledge of rocks, stood the little, heather-thatched church of Glen Tanar, known as the Black Chapel of the Moor. The inhabitants of the glen lived by cutting and dragging the wood of the vast forest to the Dee, growing turnips and potatoes on their small plots of land, and selling goats' milk to consumptives sojourning from Montrose or Aberdeen and beyond.

They lived, too, by illicitly distilling and smuggling whisky; and many a cask, in panniers on the backs of ponies, was stealthily transported by night from Glen Tanar to the waiting boatmen on the Dee, for delivery in Aberdeen. Coffins did not always contain corpses. Sometimes, excise men passed a funeral procession headed towards the river, little knowing, as they doffed their hats in respect to the black-garbed mourners following the horse-drawn hearse, that the coffin was full of whisky.

William Hall would have visited Glen Tanar periodically to inspect and select which trees he wanted and perhaps partake of an illicit dram or two of whisky with the old Earl of Aboyne, from whom he leased the Glen Tanar estate, conscious that, as a Lowland Scot, he did not speak the soft Gaelic of the kilted clan chief, as his father had.

The Wood Floaters

As soon as possible after felling, the bark was removed, whether the tree had been girdled or not; the branches were lopped, and the trunk was sawn into scantling sizes. The method used was called quarter sawing, by which the trunk was first cut into quarters and then sawn diagonally, and the scantlings were floated the thirty-odd miles down the River Dee to Aberdeen.

The wood was cut by hand and hauled by horse and cart to the river bank. The drag roads through the glen, like the Fir Mounth road, were rough in the extreme, obstructed by huge boulders left behind in the Ice Age and pitted by deep pot holes, which were filled with water after rain. It took up to ten hours to transport six loads of wood a distance of under a mile to the river. It took days to transport a load from the furthest reaches of the glen. The road was precipitous in places, varying from harness-straining slopes uphill to sharp, chain-snapping gradients downhill. The men leading the horses were always in danger of being crushed when the weight of the huge tree trunks propelled the carts too precipitously down slopes, or of losing the loads when the chains snapped when going uphill.

With the scantlings delivered to the river bank, the woodcutters'

A raft of scantlings.

job had finished; the floating of the timber was the responsibility of contractors, who provided ropes and poles as well as the men to float the scantling rafts.

The floating of timber could only take place in time of flood. The scantlings were laid on the banks in two rows to form a raft, thick end to thick end, and held together with a rope laced through iron rings that were bolted into each thick end. The other ends of the raft were bound together with a rope, laced to thin branches, to hold them in position. (The American system of logs being floated singly was not used in Scotland because of the danger of damage to bridges in swift currents.) When the floods came, the rafts were pushed into the river and floated down to Aberdeen, controlled by three men using guiding ropes and poles.

★

The Dee rises in the Wells of Dee, a spring on Ben Braeriach, in the Cairngorms, at a height of over four thousand feet. Fed by numerous streams and burns, it cascades turbulently from the mountains that flank its upper reaches and is navigable only by barges and small craft. To the west of Braemar, it forms the cascade called the Linn of Dee. The Braemar hills on either bank rise to three thousand feet, to where castles and hunting lodges mark royal forests. In places, stone circles, cairns and tumuli bear witness to other kingdoms, long vanished. Rapid and turbulent during the first half of its course of ninety miles, the Dee broadens below Aboyne, where it receives the ice-clear Water of Tanar. Past Kincardine O'Neil and the ancient town of Banchory, where the Water of Feugh forms a cascade, overlooked by castles and *clachans*, under stone bridges and granite overhangs, it meanders past Culter and Cults to Aberdeen.

At some points along the way, rocks were blasted out of the riverbed in order to make a better passage for rafts, and dams stored water to release for the floating of the timber. Many a wood floater lost his precarious balance, fell from his raft of timbers and was drowned, taken, it was believed, by the water-kelpies, who were said to haunt the dark, deep waters of the Dee.

As the wood floaters piloted their rafts downriver to Aberdeen, their shouts and river songs could be heard echoing through the trees on either shore. Sometimes, the men stopped at a riverside inn or cottage to slake their thirsts. There were several houses of call on the banks of the Dee that the floaters used to visit for food, recreation and for drink. A stone placed outside a riverside inn with a stick or two crossed sticks at the door indicated whether customers were welcome or not, for the wood floaters were generally rough, hard-drinking men.

Three years before *Mimosa* was built, an eye-witness account in *The Book of Banchory* describes the scene of wood being floated downriver on the Dee thus:

We lingered a short space and watched a succession of broad rafts, composed of tree trunks from the forests far up the river, gliding steadily along with the current. We could not but admire the dexterity with which each boatman, if we may so call him, wielded his long steering pole and guided his clumsy craft down the stream, and shot it through the archway beneath us.

Wood floating did not cease until some years after 1884, when timber was transported from the forests to the shipyards of Aberdeen by rail. As boys, William Hall's three sons witnessed the rafts of scantlings being dragged ashore. Undoubtedly, one or more of those rafts were destined to form *Mimosa*'s hull.

Seasoning and Preservation

Wood, by its very nature, is susceptible to fire, worms and dry rot. Fire occurred with great frequency during action at sea; but, with the end of the Napoleonic Wars, *Mimosa* was not likely to be embroiled in a sea battle. Worms, especially the *teredo*, also known as shipworm because of the destruction which they cause in ships' timbers or any wood immersed for long periods in the sea, were a greater danger. Existing in all seas, but especially in the tropics, the larvae make pinhole entries into the part of the wooden hull below water level, and hatch out into bi-valve molluscs that chew burrows along the grain of the wood. Their length varies from a few inches to three feet, according to the species. The greatest danger, though, was from dry rot, a fungal disease that, unless prevented, reduces wood fibres to dust; and it was found that seasoning the timber, either by natural or artificial means, helped in large measure to prevent its occurrence.

Before building could proceed, the wood was carefully piled in tiers, arranged so that there was free circulation of air around each piece, and a lump of rock salt was placed on top and left to be dissolved by the rain. This was the natural and best method of seasoning, and timber treated in this way was more durable than that seasoned by artificial methods. The time taken, however, depending on the size of the pieces of timber, varied from six to twenty-six months. To speed the process, wood was sometimes placed in a running stream, chained down so that it was entirely submerged, or soaked in a solution of metallic salts, in order to eliminate the rot-inducing sap. After two weeks of submersion, the wood was stacked in open sheds and left to dry naturally.

The seasoning and preservation completed, the scantlings were sawn into planks of the required width; they would be steamed, in vast ovens or long steam chests, to render them sufficiently pliable to be curved into ribs for the hull.

Whereas durability in oak depended upon drying out of the sap, previous to construction, masts needed the gummy resin of the Baltic pine for their suppleness and springy resilience. Pine trunks were, therefore, kept underwater, unlike oak.

The Construction

After the half model was received back from Liverpool and any refinements and modifications agreed upon, work on *Mimosa* began. Thousands of wooden pegs, called treenails, were split by hand, screw-threaded to the required inch and three-eighths diameter, and immersed in vats of brine. (The Hall shipyard was the first in Britain to use screw-threaded treenails, which had a far better holding power than the dowel.) Massive beams were fitted into precisely-cut sockets, and the great curved ribs tightly sandwiched and bolted to *Mimosa*'s frame with yard-long iron nails. The treenails were screwed into place at every foot of planking.

Mimosa's frames were of oak, on which were laid three layers of century-old larch to give her resilience as well as buoyancy. The first two layers were laid diagonally; the third was laid in the same direction as the frames. A fourth layer of larch was fitted between the fames. Felt and the best quality Baltic tar were spread between each layer, and all layers were fastened by screw-threaded treenails of oak.

Between the floors was built a permanent iron ballast, to counterbalance her tons of masts, yards, sails and rigging, without which she would keel over in the gentlest of breezes. To further guard against rot, salt was packed in the gaps between frames and in long grooves in the deck beams, before the final deck planking was laid. The decks were sloped to drain off rain and sea-water, and caulkers forced strands of tar-soaked hemp between the planks, to render the decks waterproof.

The narrow hull, like all Alexander Hall hulls, was painted dark green. The bottom was sheathed with plates of copper to prevent the accretion of barnacles, which would slow her speed, and, more importantly, to prevent the infestation of shipworm. Copper sheets were originally made of nearly pure copper, which was found to wear out too quickly and exfoliate in salt water. By experimentation with the addition of other metals, it was found that sheets made of 40 parts zinc to 60 parts copper, sometimes with a proportion of tin, reduced the rate of deterioration. Even so, the copper alloy varied in consistency from sheet to sheet, so that deterioration was not uniform: some parts had to be replaced sooner than others, so that, by the time *Mimosa* was five years old, the appearance of her copper would vary from a copper-dome green to a new-penny brightness. Puckering of the wood beneath the sheathing and loosening of the copper nails, caused by the twisting movement of the hull in heavy seas, also contributed to piecemeal deterioration. The plates, of varying thickness, were four feet by over one foot in size, the thickest being used from the bow to the waterline, the thinnest on the sides and bottom.

The galley and accommodation for the crew would be on deck, in a long, low deckhouse, most likely made of teak, the sides of which were painted with a brown varnish. The deckhouse top, the spars, the bowsprit that soared outwards and upwards from the bow and the lower masts were painted white, the topmasts, topgallants and yards were either painted dark brown, or varnished. The iron work of pumps, winches and windlass were painted black, or green to match the hull. Furniture was of the sparsest. Bunks were narrow and two-tiered, the mess table, with long benches set at each side, was plain and scrubbed. Fresh water would be pumped into a small keg from a large tank in the hold. Lighting was provided by oil lamps suspended from the ceiling; and an iron stove fuelled by coal was used for heating and cooking. Small, carved lockers would store each seaman's tools; his clothes and personal effects were kept in his own chest, which also served as a table for playing cards, or eating the daily rations of thick pea soup or salted meat. The privies were in wooden closets. The two for the seamen were in the forecastle deck, one or two for the master and higher status crew in the poop area, and all consisted of wooden seats that hung over the open sea.

Every ship had to have a figurehead, a tradition which grew out of the ancient practice of decorating bows to invoke guiding spirits to dwell in the ship, and the sweeping lines of *Mimosa*'s cutwater would look wrong without one. Her name ensured that the figurehead would be that of a female, and the name *Mimosa* was slightly exotic, suggestive of clusters of the fluffy yellow blossom found in the wild grasslands of South America, in China and above the mangrove forests in West Africa – the places to which her voyages destined her.

In the carver's shop near the wharf, William Hall would have drawn on the floor the lines of the bow, to show where *Mimosa*'s figurehead would go, and perhaps he discussed with the carver the kind of figurehead required. The carver would then have chalked his design on a block of oak, selected for its shape and size, and, with hammer, chisel and gouger, a figure would have emerged, Galatea-like, as if freed from her arboreal prison. *Mimosa*'s figurehead, her guiding spirit, approved and painted – her long, streaming hair likely painted a pale mimosa yellow, her eyes as blue as the sea – was bolted into position.

The carver was probably Robert Hall, who had carved the figureheads of other ships built in the Alexander Hall shipyard. Possibly, he was a relative of William and James Hall – a nephew, cousin or uncle, perhaps. Based on the cost of the figurehead that he had carved for William Hall's best-known ship, *Cairngorm*, a few months before, the figurehead for *Mimosa* would have cost less than £20.

Finally, the letters H M F N were carved along one of the outside beams of her hull. These four letters, which were *Mimosa*'s alone, would correspond to the four flags or pennants which, when hoisted, would identify her when at sea or coming into port.

Beta Crucis

It is likely that *Mimosa* was named, not after the delicately blossomed tree of the same name, but after the star called *Beta Crucis*, or Mimosa, one of the four stars that form the constellation known as the Southern Cross.

Three thousand times brighter than the sun and eight times larger, Mimosa is a magnificent blue-white star of such luminosity that she is, in fact, the nineteenth brightest star in the galaxy. She is a young star – a mere ten million years old – and three hundred and fifty light years distant from the earth. Dangling below her is a cluster of ruby, sapphire and topaz stars known as the Jewel Box, which vanish into a black void known as the Coal Sack. So striking is this constellation of which she forms a part that seafarers sailing into the Southern Hemisphere used to cross themselves when gazing at it. The exact origin of her name, Mimosa, is not known. It possibly derives from the Latin word for mimic or actor. Mimosa is, in fact, a double star, whose components are too close to one another to see separately.

Mimosa and her three bright sisters, named more prosaically *Alpha Crucis* or Acrux, *Gamma Crucis* or Gacrux, and *Delta Crucis* were once part of the constellation of the Centaur. So compelling were the four stars that they were noted by Ptolemy, and were known to the ancient Greeks and Chaldeans, who included them on their star maps. Hindu astronomers recorded a 'beam of crucifixion', which they named *Snia*, or *Shula*. In Biblical times, from Palestine, the four stars were just visible at the horizon and were an object of reverence. Was it Mimosa, perhaps, or one of her sisters, that guided the Wise Men to a certain stable in

Bethlehem? Over time, movement of the earth's axis brought the stars into the Southern Hemisphere; they were last seen in northern skies two thousand years ago, at about the time of Christ's crucifixion.

Roman astrologers named the four stars, visible then from Alexandria, *Thronos Caesaris*, in honour of the emperor Augustus. Amerigo Vespucci called the constellation of the New World *La Mandorla* – The Almond – which is also the word used in Italian art for the *vestica piscis*, the oblong glory surrounding saints ascending into heaven. It was not until the 16th century, however, that the astral quartet was separated from the Centaur and given the name *Crux Australis,* or Southern Cross, or simply Crux.

When Cabral discovered Brazil in 1500, he named it Vera Cruz – True Cross – which was later changed to Santa Cruz – Holy Cross. The first map of the new continent named South America as *Terra Sancte Crucis* – the Land of the Holy Cross.

It was primarily for the rich trade in the Land of the Holy Cross for which *Mimosa* was constructed, to which she was destined to sail on twenty of her twenty-seven voyages – under the star after which she was likely named.

The Ship and Launch

Mimosa was a three-masted sailing ship of just over 447 ton, by the New Measurement. She was carvel-built, to allow for a tighter hull and faster speed, with imitation galleries. It was customary, then, to pay 50% of the purchase price in cash, the rest in bills of exchange dated four to six months later. Robert Vining and William Killey paid a total of £5,916, or £12 per ton, in instalments as construction progressed, and the work was subjected to periodic survey examination. The final payment was made on delivery to Liverpool. She was Alexander Hall & Sons' 187th ship.[2]

Mimosa was diminutive, in comparison with the 2000-ton American clippers, the undisputed queens of the seas, built to attain astonishing speeds and to navigate the treacherous seas around Cape Horn. *Mimosa* would never achieve the speed of a Yankee clipper, but she would be better than her stately American cousins in lighter winds and, if required to do so, could be counted upon to make the run from Shanghai or Foochow to London in a little over a hundred days – a princess of the seas rather than a queen.

The captain for her first five voyages was a young master mariner in his early thirties, Thomas Kemp. Upon her completion, he and his young wife, Sarah, travelled by train from Liverpool to Aberdeen, to inspect the ship that he had been selected to captain, just three days earlier.

Any ship launch in Footdee was an occasion for celebration, and *Mimosa*'s launch, on Tuesday, June 21, 1853, was no exception. Children were excused from school since the schoolmaster also wanted to witness the launch. Women left the baiting of lines and gutting of fish and put on their finery. Fishing boats were beached. William Hall, his employees, their wives and children were dressed in their Sunday best, and the shipyard was decorated with ribbons and bunting.

Greater than the pervading atmosphere of celebration was anticipation of the revelation of her name, kept a closely-guarded secret even from the men who built her, until the moment of her ceremonial baptism. She must have looked slight, cradled between the two layers of beams that supported her underbelly, bare of the masts that would more than treble her height, her figurehead decorated with ribbons. Expert hands stroked her ribs, feeling for any weakness that would imperil her seaworthiness, and her gleaming brass work was given a final, unnecessary rub with a cloth.

Sarah Kemp, expecting her first child, was helped onto the railed platform under the backwards-facing figurehead. When Thomas Kemp and the rest of the launching party were assembled beside her, James Hall handed Sarah the bottle of wine, decorated with rosettes, dangling from a rope. A long, triangular flag tied to one of the masts revealed her name, *Mimosa*, to the cheering onlookers and the shipyard employees. The secret was out at last. The bottle of wine was raised, and the crowd held their collective breath in case the bottle was not swung with sufficient force to break it, which would have marked *Mimosa* as a doomed ship. There was a shattering of glass as the bottle smashed against her hull. The crowd cheered; James and William Hall beamed their relief.

At a nod from William Hall, one of the of yard men smashed the blocks of wood supporting her keel, and, borne by her own weight, *Mimosa* slipped down the thickly-greased incline, stern first, into the water with an enormous splash, temporary braces keeping her rudder from swinging to one side and breaking off. There was not much room for launching at the shipyard, and there was danger of *Mimosa* crashing against the rocks on the far side of the bank. There was a spluttering of sparks from the tautening of cables and a splintering of timber into matchwood. Anchors, dragging through the gravel, slowed her progress, and the restraining cables prevented her from hitting the river bank, where men stood by with long poles ready to bring her to a standstill before her stern touched land. Anxiously, William Hall shouted to the men on the bank, while Thomas Kemp, James Hall and some of the shipyard employees stood on deck, anxious to see for themselves how she took to the water.

Once *Mimosa* had been successfully launched, the young carpenter apprentices were chased, laughing, and thrown three times into the water, in a ritual that replaced human sacrifice by drowning. The spilt wine smashed against her hull represented the blood of a bound victim, crushed beneath the vessel as it slid into the water, sacrificed to appease a vindictive sea god. The office boys, warily watching the immersions, quickly denuded *Mimosa* of her ribbons and rosettes to keep as an exchange for a kiss or a promise of a kiss at the next Hogmanay ball.

To celebrate her launch, William and James Hall would have entertained Thomas Kemp and his young wife in a hotel in Aberdeen, while the shipyard staff celebrated her launch in the mould loft, temporarily converted to a banqueting hall and gaily decorated with flags. In both places, a toast would have been raised, to wish *Mimosa* well.

The *Aberdeen Journal* reported the occasion on the following day.

Yesterday there was launched from the building yard of Messrs. Hall a splendid ship-rigged vessel, named the Mimosa. Her measurement is 447 tons, New Measurement, and 540, Old Measurement. The Mimosa is the property of Liverpool owners and is the third vessel which Messrs. Hall have built for the same parties. She is intended for the South American trade and is to be commanded by Mr. Kemp, a gentleman of long experience, whose fair partner gave the vessel her name. The Mimosa is a really splendid ship and promises to be worthy of her builders. She at present lies at Provost Blaikie's Quay.[3]

In the riggers' wharf to which she was towed following her launch *Mimosa* was fitted with her masts and the miles of rigging needed to support her acres of sail. She was ready to leave the shipyard for whatever awaited her in her sea-going life.

Leaving Aberdeen

On July 5, 1853, *Mimosa* left Aberdeen, with Thomas Kemp at the helm, and a crew who had signed on in Aberdeen. Originally, she was to be sailed at the Halls' expense, 'from Aberdeen to Liverpool and to be moored in dock and the anchors taken on board to the satisfaction of the master.'[4]

She did not, however, sail to Liverpool at all. In what appeared to be a last moment decision on the part of her owners, her destination was changed. Evidently a cargo closer to Aberdeen was procured for her, thus saving the Halls the cost of delivery. Instead of heading north towards the fast-flowing tides and treacherous currents of the Pentland Firth, it was decided that she would sail south along the east coast of Scotland, past Stonehaven, Montrose, the Firth of Tay and the gaping mouth of the Firth of Finch, to North Shields, a seaport in Northumberland lying on the north bank of the River Tyne, some seven miles east of Newcastle, that is surrounded by vast salt flats for which both Shields – North and South – are known.

Farmers in the fields overlooking the sea and the fishermen in their boats gazed in wonder at the new clipper, smaller than most, her dark green hull slicing the waves as precisely as a tailor's scissors cutting cloth, the tresses of her female figurehead streaming in stylized abandon in the salt-laden wind, her painted eyes, bluer than the sea or the sky above, gazing straight ahead. Thomas Kemp, with Sarah at his side, watched anxiously to see how *Mimosa* took to the waters of the North Sea as she sailed down the coasts of Scotland and Northumberland, noting how her sails filled and what speeds she attained in the varying wind speeds.

The coast is rocky and dangerous; but *Mimosa* anchored safely in the harbour, enclosed by a north and a south pier, to load her first cargo. On July 22, at the Custom House in Newcastle, Thomas Kemp was formally endorsed as master.

Mimosa's first crew was discharged and another crew signed on for the voyage to Rio de Janeiro, Montevideo and Buenos Aires, to a final port of discharge at Bristol, that commenced on July 28, 1853, just over a month after her launch. Her cargo was probably salt, needed in vast quantities for the salting of meat and the preservation of hides. Sarah likely returned to Liverpool by train from Newcastle, to await the birth of her child.

Meanwhile, in an office in Liverpool, Robert Vining was arranging to give James Hall the final payment on his newest clipper, and had invited his partner to partake of a celebratory glass of sherry. Much would be expected of *Mimosa* by her Liverpool owners. Even more would be demanded.

Part II

The Liverpool Owners

The flood tide of Liverpool commerce had now set in, and rushed on with ever increasing force.

J A Picton, *Memorials of Liverpool.*

Liverpool

In July of 1853, when *Mimosa* was entered into the books of her Liverpool owners, Liverpool was the second most populous city in Britain, with more than one hundred thousand people per square mile; only London's population was greater. More foreign and overseas trade was done in Liverpool than in any other city in the world, and it far surpassed London in commercial aggression. It controlled the world's trade in sugar, salt and palm oil, and led the world market in cotton and grain.

It was a city of stark contrasts. Many lived in luxury that rivalled princes'. Others eked out existences as warehouse and shipping clerks, chandlers, rope makers, anchor smiths, sail makers, wheelwrights, soap boilers, lime burners, herring curers, labourers and coopers, which the great port demanded. Brothels and gin houses proliferated, and there were miles upon miles of streets and mean alleys, that had no sewage disposal, sun or air. For most of the population, living in overcrowded slums and airless courtyards or underground cellars, water was a luxury, and health a gamble that many lost. Cholera and typhoid fever were rampant; infant mortality was high; and starvation, for many, hovered not far away. As the poverty-stricken flooded in from all parts of England, Wales and Ireland to find work in the docks, long ribbons of terraced houses and tenements were built across former fields and heath lands; and crowded courts and bleak back-to-back houses changed for ever the tranquil scattering of villages and hamlets.

In the 8th century, colonies of Norsemen settled on both sides of the Mersey, at the mouth of which was a large pool or sea lake; and a possible derivation of Liverpool is from the Norse *Hlithar-pollr*, the pool of the slopes. The bottle-shaped pool, narrowest at its elongated mouth, was a small inlet where ships could harbour in safety from the swift currents, treacherous sandbanks and shifting channels of the Mersey estuary. The pressure of water into and out of the great pool created strong currents and high tides that rise from fifteen to twenty-one feet. Further eastwards, some two miles from the shore, bogs and marshes made commerce with the hinterland difficult and extremely hazardous. At the time of the Domesday survey, Liverpool was so unimportant that it was not even mentioned, and was first marked on a map of Britain in 1331, where it was named as Lytherpoole. When King John, having lost his Angevin possessions in France, turned his attention west and north, he created the Borough of Liverpool, a place better situated than the ancient port of Chester from which to launch his attacks on Ireland and Wales. All ships belonged to the king; they were mainly deployed for fishing, and there were few merchant ships. In the Middle Ages, Liverpool lay on the fringe of the known world, but could not compete with ports like Venice or Genoa, which lay in the centre of that world. Trade developed only slowly, with the export of fish and wool to France and Spain, and the imports of butter and linen from Ireland; and, in 1360, the Black Death carried off a large part of the population. After the discovery of America, however, Liverpool lay mid-way between the Old and New Worlds, and her position on the western coastline of Europe put her on a par with the ports of Bordeaux, Bilboa and Cadiz.

An increase in commerce came at the end of the 17th century, with the manufacturing industry of south Lancashire, locally produced salt from Cheshire and from Liverpool itself, and the opening of the American and West Indian trade. By the end of the century, the population of Liverpool had increased to five thousand. Trade was chiefly with the colonies in Virginia and the West Indies, from which tobacco and sugar were imported. The harbour became too small to accommodate the increase in shipping, and, in 1715, a dock, known as the Old Dock – the first of its kind, which was later copied for the East and West India Docks on the Thames – was built, with flood gates to dam the water so that ships could remain afloat at low tide.

Among the first ships to use the Old Dock were vessels used to transport indigent whites as slaves to the New World, who, however, were inadequte in physical strength and numbers to meet the needs for manual workers.

By their connection with trade with the West Indies, Liverpool merchants entered the African slave trade, their ships sailing first to the west coast of Africa with 'Manchester goods' to be exchanged for slaves, who were transported to the West Indies where they were sold, the proceeds being brought back to Liverpool as cargoes of sugar, raw cotton and rum. Before its abolition in 1807, five-sixths of the African slave trade was centred in Liverpool.

As one source of wealth closed, many more opened and, with the abolition of slavery, Liverpool merchants looked for trade in new markets. While maintaining traditional trade with the Baltic and the Mediterranean, Liverpool's main sources of commerce from shipping derived from

Transatlantic trade in cotton, sugar and palm oil. With independence from Spain and Portugal, new markets emerged in South America. By the middle of the 19th century, Liverpool merchants were trading with the whole world, carrying cargoes between North and South America, the West Indies, the Mediterranean and Black Sea, Africa, Australia, Russia, India and China.

In 1853, Liverpool was the largest port in the world, through which 40% of the world's trade was being carried by its ships. It ranked as a financial centre that was second only to London, and its commerce extended to every corner of the globe. Ships and barques, brigantines, schooners and steam tugs were in constant movement. Lofty masts disappeared into low-lying clouds. Fifty ships might dock in any one day, three hundred sometimes left on any one tide.

The docks and basins, the names of which were inspired by the royal family, military men, politicians and local dignitaries, extended over six and a half miles along the Mersey estuary. (The Huskisson dock alone had an area of more than fifteen acres and possessed the widest dock gates in the world.) There were twenty-seven miles of wet, half-tide and graving, or dry, docks;[5] and the landing stage was the largest floating structure in the world, and still the need for new docks increased. The Clarence, with its basin and two graving docks, where *Mimosa* would be refitted for her voyage to Patagonia twelve years later, opened in September 1830. Designed for steamships, the Clarence was situated well away from the rest of the dock system, since a single spark from a funnel could cause a raging fire among the densely-packed wooden ships in port. Warehouses of four or more storeys, covering hundreds of acres, rose in colonnaded splendour, the tobacco warehouse alone occupying some thirty-six acres. The grain silos were the largest in the world. Stacking yards for timber extended for miles. Bonded warehouses stored the world's finest wines and spirits. Horse-drawn carts and wagons continually shifted goods from quaysides to warehouses, from warehouses to quaysides. Crimps delivered men, drunk or drugged, from taverns onto seagoing ships. Emigrants, housed in flea- and rat-ridden hostels, awaited transportation in ships. Paying passengers boarded or disembarked from liners, coming from or bound to New York, Philadelphia, Bombay, Sydney, Hong Kong or Montreal, while ship owners and merchants, dressed in tailcoats and silk hats, met in the Liverpool Exchange to discuss the latest news and transact business.

Liverpool merchants, like their counterparts in London, St Petersburg and Bristol, had commercial interests in every part of the world and were renowned for their business acumen. Their large, imposing houses were in the best parts of the city: Sefton, Princes Park and Mossley Hill, and little was skimped in the building and furnishing of them. Despite outward signs of wealth, they lived simple, God-fearing lives as staunch Anglicans, Presbyterians or Quakers, and involved themselves in public and civic duties. They owned, or attempted to own, their own family pews in the most prestigious churches. They patronized the arts and involved themselves in public works and civic duties. They were self confident, prosperous, imaginative in matters relating to commerce, granite-hard and ruthless in business, and upheld the strict values of the middle-class Victorian gentleman. Their wealth was rarely inherited. They worked hard for it and worked even harder to keep it; and the gap between vast wealth and abject poverty widened.

The wealth and importance of Liverpool was in its full tide, and one more ship was about to take a part in its maritime trade.

Registration

On July 19, 1853, *Mimosa*'s name, dimensions, tonnage and description were entered in the *Customs and Excise Register* in Liverpool. The huge, leather-bound register, with its thick parchment pages that were large enough to record, over the years, a ship's seagoing life, was so heavy that it could not be easily lifted. She is described as being *'Built at Aberdeen in the County of Aberdeen in the present year One Thousand Eight Hundred and Fifty-Three as appears by a certificate under the hand of Alexander Hall and Company the Builders, dated 27 June 1853.'* The name of the surveying officer was James McCallum, tide surveyor at the Port of Aberdeen.[6]

Until 1868, only ships needing underwriting had to be registered, for the purposes of insurance; and Vining & Killey did not list *Mimosa* in *Lloyd's Register*. The Treaty of Tien Tsin of 1868, designed to stop piracy, which was prevalent especially in the South China Seas, instituted registration of all ships. A registration certificate from the ship's home port, together with a custom's manifest of the cargo from the port of lading, and ship's articles or agreements, signed by the crew at the start of the voyage, enabled legitimate ships to be distinguished from those of pirates, thus protecting a ship and its owner from arbitrary arrest on suspicion.

The value of a ship lay in the weight of cargo it was designed to carry, and it was taxed accordingly. A formula, whereby the volume of a ship's hull could be converted into the equivalent weight in tons of sea water, referred to as Builder's Tonnage or Builder's Old Measure, was used until 1854; the new standard of measurement was referred to as New Measure. By the Old Measure, the hull's depth below the waterline could be dangerously increased by excess cargo weight, without increasing the tonnage figure, and, consequently, the harbour dues and taxes upon which tonnage was calculated. The assessment of a safe load was generally left to the discretion of the owners, who frequently put the safety of their ships at risk by packing additional cargo that would not be taxed and would, therefore, give a higher rate of net profit. (In 1840, *Lloyd's Register* recorded an average of 1.5 ships per day lost because of overloading.)

Although the new formula was not compulsory until the year after *Mimosa* was built, William Hall calculated her tonnage on the New Measure (NM). Her tonnage is also given in Old Measure (OM).

Mimosa was registered as a ship ('ship-rigged') having three masts and a female figurehead. Her registration number was 1973. Her tonnage was registered at 447 tons by the new scale of measurement (NM), 540 tons by the old (OM). Her length from fore to stern was 139 9/10 ft., her breadth amidships 25 5/10 ft., the depth in the hold 15 6/10 ft.

Daniel Green, a forty-seven-year-old master mariner of Liverpool, who held shares in her and was, therefore, a joint-owner with Vining and Killey, was listed as master. Born in Essex in 1806, he obtained his master's certificate in London, just three years prior to *Mimosa*'s construction.[7] Since the days of the East India Company, captains were appointed to ships during their construction so that they could superintend the stages of the building. As her designated master, Daniel Green would certainly have superintended *Mimosa*'s construction in Aberdeen, perhaps suggesting modifications or insisting upon refinements to William Hall's design. Robert Vining and William Killey would have shown him the half-model of *Mimosa*'s hull, which he would have scrutinized with a practised eye.

Three days after her registration, on July 22, Daniel Green was officially replaced by Thomas Kemp. Daniel Green was given command of another ship – *Urania*, on the Liverpool to Australia run. Why he relinquished the opportunity of sailing *Mimosa* to her first destination is not known. In any case, he remained one of *Mimosa*'s joint-owners until almost the end of her seagoing life.

The Partnership

Mimosa's cost, together with the expenses, profits or losses that would accrue from her voyages, was divided among several subscribing owners, who owned a total of sixty-four equal shares between them. By the ancient Laws of Oléron, an island some eighteen miles in length lying off the west coast of France that had formerly been part of the duchy of Aquitaine, the fractional shareholding of a vessel became characteristic of all Genoese and Venetian shipping in the 12th century. It enabled merchants and ship owners to spread their risks, when losses of ships and their cargoes by storm, piracy or bad navigation could spell ruin. Insurance was expensive and could not always be secured. Mortgage, too, was an unsatisfactory expedient, for the interest rate required was high.

Every ship had a different group of owners and was a separate venture. By owning shares in several ships, instead of in one, and by offering shares in a ship to other merchants, retired or active master mariners keen to invest their savings in the kind of enterprise they knew best, relatives or friends, or even tradesmen with connections to shipping as suppliers of stores, the profits would be less, but so would the risk of financial loss. In Britain, the Merchant Shipping Act of 1854 settled on the sixty-fourth as the invariable division in ownership of British ships, and allowed only one owner to be registered, his decisions being binding on the other shareholders.

Ship owners' profits were wholly dependent upon the skills and honesty of the master, the rise and fall of freight rates, and the always-present risks of storms, piracy and shipwrecks. The costs of operating the ship were borne by its owners, in proportion to the number of their shares. Ship ownership was a partnership often of ten or twelve individuals, brought together through mutual acquaintances, or through an advertisement in a local newspaper, who were content to leave the management of the ship to one or two partners, who, like Robert Vining and William Killey, had initiated the purchase of a particular vessel.

Shareholders in a ship were usually – although, not always – merchants, and shares were freely transferable by a bill of sale, without the necessity of consent from the other part-owners. Just three months notice in writing was sufficient to dissolve a partnership. Shareholders enjoyed access to markets far beyond the confines of their provincial towns, and this provided them with a vicarious sense of adventure. They were often entertained on board, prior to the ship's first voyage, sometimes at the commencement of each long voyage, and on the presentation of periodic accounts. Such gatherings gave them a chance to see their ship and to become acquainted with one another, especially when new shareholders had joined the partnership.

The subscribing owners had no real say in the management of *Mimosa*. If she was well managed, they needed only to meet at the end of every voyage and sign the account book, to signify their acceptance of its accuracy and collect their dividends.[8]

Robert Vining and William Killey

Robert Vining was forty-six when he formed a partnership with William Killey and became joint-owner of *Mimosa*. He was then at the peak of his commercial abilities. Before this, he had been a partner in trading with Thomas McTear, with whom he had owned two ships, also built by Alexander Hall & Sons – *Bonita* and *Reindeer*, the latter one of the finest ships of its kind. He was, in fact, still legally in partnership with Thomas McTear, when he formed the partnership with William Killey. He had links with other Liverpool merchants, powerful men like Jervis Whardley, for whom Alexander Hall & Sons were also building ships, and who owned shares in *Reindeer*.

Robert Vining [9]

Until the beginning of the 19th century, the term 'ship owner' was not in use and does not appear in the 18th century directories of Bristol, Liverpool or Newcastle, where ship-owning merchants were described as 'Turkey merchants', 'Russia merchants', 'India merchants', etc. Only when the Industrial Revolution was changing the scale of British commerce did ship-owning become an occupation in its own right. Most, like Robert Vining, did business in the Northern and Southern Hemispheres, especially the latter; and the greatest asset for any merchant were his connections in his home port and in the countries in which he traded. Competition for cargoes was fierce; and the well-connected merchant with a reputation for fair dealing had an advantage.

Before his interests turned to shipping, Robert Vining had been one of the founders of the Liverpool newspaper, *The Daily Albion*, and was a known philanthropist. He was, for a time, city councillor and alderman, and had links with some of the most influential men in Liverpool. He was one of the subscribers to the publication of Thomas Baines' *History of the Commerce and Town of Liverpool and of the Rise of Manufacturing Industry in the Adjoining Counties*, which was published by the author in Liverpool in 1852, and was clearly attuned to the immense commercial possibilities for shipping in Liverpool. He tried, unsuccessfully, to purchase a family pew in the Anglican church at Walton-on-Hill, upon the death of the original pew-owner. The previous owner's son, although he resided in London, refused to sell. Vining had a house in St Ann's Hill, in Anfield, which had a garden that backed onto a park, coach house and stabling for six horses. He was undoubtedly wealthy.

William Killey was, perhaps, the person who had most to do with the administrative running of *Mimosa*. A former master mariner, he had contacts with chandlers, ship owners and other master mariners. It was he who would have appointed Thomas Kemp as master, perhaps on the recommendation of Daniel Green, and he decided all practical matters relating to *Mimosa*. William Killey kept the accounts, paid the wages of the master and crew, and prepared the statements periodically issued to the shareholders.

In 1853, William Killey owned shares in *Bonita*, of which, in 1848, he was the ship's first master. James Browne Killey, obviously a relative of William Killey, owned eight shares in the same ship and was listed as a merchant. William Killey was connected by marriage to George Deane, one of *Mimosa*'s first subscribing partners. George Deane had a business partner, Frederick Youle, an Englishman with commercial interests in Pernambuco, the largest sugar-producing area in Brazil, who also held shares in *Bonita*.

George Deane's association with Frederick Youle was of undoubted benefit to Robert Vining and William Killey and was possibly one of their reasons for directing their commercial and trading interests and their ships to Brazil and, indirectly, the reason for *Mimosa*'s construction.

The partnership between William Killey and Robert Vining was formed just prior to the construction of *Mimosa*, while Robert Vining was still in partnership with Thomas McTear. William Killey demonstrated a canny sense of when to sell his shares in *Bonita* and when to buy them back, which must have impressed Robert Vining sufficiently to suggest that they become partners in a new ship, built principally for the South American trade.

Correspondence between himself and Robert Vining remained strictly formal and confined to business matters, William Killey invariably addressing Robert Vining respectfully as Sir, throughout the years of their partnership. Killey was the accountant, familiar with ships and the sea; Robert Vining was the merchant with wealth and influential friends. William Killey was the man who decided when they should sell their various ships, and it is likely that Robert Vining relied upon his judgement. It was William Killey, not Robert Vining, who determined *Mimosa*'s ultimate fate.

The Transactions[10]

1853

In 1853, upon her delivery to Liverpool from Aberdeen, Robert VINING and William KILLEY owned between them 8 shares in *Mimosa*.

Daniel GREEN, Master Mariner of Liverpool also had 8 shares.

George DEANE, a merchant of Liverpool, owned 16 shares.

Robert RILEY, a gentleman of Manchester, owned 8 shares.

John WOOD, a merchant of Glossop, Chester, owned 16 shares.

John BRADBURY, a merchant of Saddleworth, County of York, owned 8 shares.

1854

On 17 April 1854, George Deane transferred 4 shares to Richard

GREEN, a ship owner of Liverpool (possibly a relative of Daniel Green, or of the famous Richard Green of the Blackwall Line of ships in London).

On September 12, 1854, John Bradbury transferred his 8 shares to James BROADBENT, a merchant of Carr, County of York.

Upon becoming bankrupt, James Broadbent's 8 shares were transferred to Francis SHAW BUCKLEY, a banker of Uppermill, Saddleworth, County of York.

1855

On July 14 1855, George Deane, being adjudged bankrupt on November 13, 1854, transferred his remaining 12 shares to the following three men:

James CASENOVE, the appointed assignee.

James SMITH, a banker.

Samuel MONSDALE MELLOR, a Liverpool merchant.

On July 23, 1855, the 12 shares owned by Cazenove, Smith and Monsdale Mellor were purchased by Robert VINING and William KILLEY, giving them a total of 20 shares and making them principal shareholders in *Mimosa*.

1856

On August 8, 1856, Francis Shaw Buckley died, and his 8 shares were transferred back to James BROADBENT of Carr, York, giving him a total of 16 shares.

1858

On April 10, 1858, Robert Riley of Manchester died, and his 8 shares were acquired by Sydney JESSOP, a steel manufacturer from Sheffield, County of York, and William BINGHAM, a draper from Manchester.

1860

On April 5, 1860, Sydney Jessop and William Bingham sold their 8 shares to Henry HOLLAND of Liverpool, a merchant.

On May 25, 1860 Robert Vining and William Killey sold 4 of their 20 shares to Trevanion HUGO, a master mariner of Liverpool.

1863

On December 6, 1863, Trevanion Hugo died and his appointed executors, Thomas HUGO, a ship chandler, and Charles HOWELL, an accountant, both of Liverpool, became owners of the shares.

On May 27, 1864, Thomas Hugo and Charles Howell sold their shares to Emma HUGO of Liverpool, Trevanion Hugo's widow.

1865

On December 20, 1865, Emma Hugo sold the shares back to Thomas HUGO and to James HUGHES, a plumber from Liverpool.

1866

On May 3, 1866, Henry Holland died and left his 8 shares to Eliza HAMILTON of Notting Hill, London.

1867

On December 21, 1867, Eliza Hamilton mortgaged her shares for £282 to Charles WIGG, a merchant, and Henry William EDDIS, an accountant, both of Liverpool.

1869

On December 16, 1869, John Wood of Glossop, who had held 16 shares in *Mimosa*, died, and the administration of his shares was granted to his widow, Emma WOOD, by the Court of Probate in Derby.

On December 27, 1869, James Broadbent, who had held 8 shares, died, and John BROADBENT WOOD, a merchant of Carr (possibly a nephew) was appointed executor and administered his shares.

1870

On March 4, 1870, Thomas Hugo and James Hughes sold their

4 shares to John GRAY of 130 Kensington Park, London, a master mariner.

On November 30, 1870, Charles Wigg and Henry William Eddis, who held 8 shares under mortgage, sold their shares to William KILLEY.

On December 2, 1870, Emma Wood sold her 16 shares to William KILLEY.

On December 30, 1870, John Broadbent Wood sold his recently acquired 8 shares to William KILLEY.

1871

On January 30, 1871, Daniel Green, who held 8 shares, and Richard Green, who held 4, sold their shares to William KILLEY.

On February 8, 1871, John Gray sold his 4 shares to William KILLEY.

Finally, on February 15, 1871, William KILLEY bought out his partner, Robert Vining, by acquiring all 16 shares which they held jointly, making him sole owner of *Mimosa*.

The Painting

A painting of *Mimosa* was commissioned. It is not known who commissioned it or who the artist was, since the painting is unsigned. It is of the English School of marine painting, a style that was well established by 1850 and lasted until 1880. The canvas measures 71 x 43 cms. (28 x 17 inches) and depicts *Mimosa*, viewed from the starboard side, entering Sydney harbour between the North and South Heads. Her flags show that she is requesting a pilot to guide her into port. The crew are busy at their tasks. Other clippers – no less than nine – are seen in the distance, suggesting commerce and profit, of which *Mimosa* was then clearly a part. Owners had pride in their ships. They liked to have portraits of them; and if it was not, as was most probable, Robert Vining who commissioned the painting, it might have been William Killey, or one of merchants who held shares in her.

Such was the number of ships in the mid 19th century that an artist could support himself and his family by painting portraits of them. Often, the artists themselves had served at sea, had been apprenticed to ship owners or shipbuilders, or had grown up in seaports, for they had an intuitive knowledge of ships and seafaring. They understood the intricacies of rigging, the importance of flags, the set of sails in particular weathers, the perspective of hull and deck; and were able to depict accurately the movement of waves created by hulls of varying shapes.

Paintings commissioned by owners or master mariners had to be accurate as well as decorative. Sailing safely into a busy port, near a recognizable headland, under clear blue skies, or anchored on waves that resembled ruched silk, preparing to unload, were settings which appealed to ship owners and merchant shareholders. Understandably, storms and wrecks were not popular settings. Neither was the loneliness of the open sea, especially at night, or the harsh reality of working life on ship or in port. Full daylight, up until the late afternoon, indicating a full day's work, was preferable to sunrise or sunset.

It is wholly improbable that the portrait of *Mimosa* was actually executed at sea, and there is no evidence that she ever sailed to Australia, although many clippers on the Liverpool to China tea routes sailed via Sydney if they had cargo to carry there. Unless he was a well known artist, who was directly commissioned to paint *Mimosa*'s portrait, he would have been one of scores of artists who made their living by daily visiting the Liverpool port for orders. Seeing *Mimosa* in dock, the artist could have found out the names of her owners from the crew or port officials. Then, he might have taken a few preliminary sketches to the office of Robert Vining or William Killey, or one of her shareholders, who could have suggested the setting that most appealed to them. The size of the canvas would have been determined by the room in which the painting was to be hung, and a price would have been agreed upon, to be paid on completion of the painting, probably ten or fifteen shillings. The artist would probably have used a model of a three-masted ship, to ensure the correct representation of the rigging.

The painting, apart from the written record of her voyages and statistics, is the only tangible testimony to *Mimosa* that has endured.

Mimosa

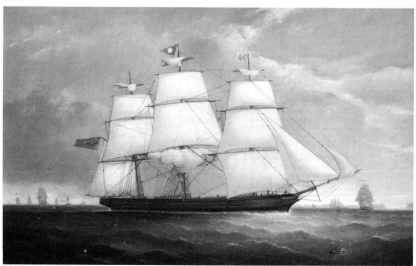

Part III

The China Voyages

I did send for a cup of tee, a China drink, of which I never had drunk before.
Samuel Pepys.

The Tea Trade

The tea plant (*Thea sinensis*) is an evergreen, which, in its natural state, grows to a height of fifteen to thirty feet. By pruning and plucking, it is restricted to a low bushy shrub, which produces a flush of leaves, the gathering of which is called a crop, about every forty days. The leaves are thick, smooth and leathery. The flowers are fragrant and consist of five white petals. The fruit is hard-shelled, like a hazelnut.

There are three primary types of tea: green, oolong and black. All three types can be harvested from the same bush, the difference between them being in the processing and fermentation. The green teas are the Gunpowders, Imperials, Hysons and Twankeys. The black teas are the Boheas, Congous, Souchongs, Keemuns, Ningchows and Ichangs. They vary in quality and taste depending on the region, South China teas being different from North China teas. The Oolongs, like the Souchongs, are sometimes scented with jasmine flowers. Depending on the type of tea, the leaves are either allowed to wilt naturally, by spreading them on trays, or heating them in pans over charcoal fires, to inhibit the oxidizing enzymes; and the treated leaves are then rolled, fermented and dried.

The origins of the use of tea as a beverage are ancient. It is thought to have been drunk in China since at least 2737 BC, where, according to legend, it was discovered by the emperor Chin Nung, or Shen Nung, a scholar and herbalist, who drank only boiled water, until a few leaves from the tea tree under which he was sitting fell into his pot of simmering water. There is, however, no written reference to tea until the third century BC. Grown first in the wild, the leaves were pounded, mixed with plum juice to bind the particles together, and compressed into a brick-shaped cake, which could be boiled in water. In later centuries, it was ground into a fine powder and whipped into a green froth. Finally, it was steeped as leaf tea in boiled water.

In whatever form, whether cake, powder or leaf, Chinese traders took it over mountain passes and old silk roads, to Tibet and India. As Europeans voyaged to the East in search of spices, they also discovered the refreshing *tcha*. When the links between China and Portugal were established in the early 16th century, tea does not appear to have been of any interest to traders, although the Portuguese acquired a taste for it through their depot at Macao, established in 1557. No reference to tea is found in European literature until 1559, when a Venetian, Giambattista Ramusio, seeking supplies of spices and silk, evidently tasted the fragrant beverage and found it sufficiently pleasant to refer to it in his *Delle navagatione e viaggi*. The earliest mention of tea by an Englishman was in a letter from an agent of the East India Company in Japan, Richard Wickham, who had been offered *chaw* from a silver porringer and liked it sufficiently to ask for more. It was not until the latter part of the 17th century, however, that tea began to be known in England.

The Dutch East India Company shipped tea first to Holland, via Java. It was then transported to London, the first merchant selling it there in 1657. The following year, Thomas Garraway, a general merchant with a shop in Exchange Alley, in the City of London, advertised 'that excellent China drink called by the Chineans *tcha*, by other nations *tay*, alias *tee*', which began to be sold in the 'cophee' shops in London. It was drunk from a dish, and was so exorbitantly expensive that it was used only for gifts for princes and grandees and as an exotic delicacy when the entertainment was sufficiently lavish for the hosts to be able to afford it. Four years after Garraway's enthusiastic endorsement, Catherine of Braganza brought, as part of her dowry to her marriage with Charles II, a chest of China tea, and established the fashion of drinking tea at Court. Ladies began to partake of tea in their homes, while men drank it in the company of bankers, politicians, writers and poets, in coffee houses such as Twining's, off the Strand, or Lloyd's, in the City. The East India Company decided to purchase tea direct from China, and, in 1689, made their first shipment. When the coffee houses fell into disrepute, covered tea gardens appeared, such as those at Vauxhall and Ranelagh, where men and women, accompanied by their children, could walk, listen to a band or watch a firework display as they drank tea, which was still expensive.

For several years, the quantity of tea imported was small and exclusively of the finer sorts. In the 18th century, the use of tea in England and its colonies rapidly increased and, by 1800, tea was being drunk by all classes in England as an alternative to ale. Britain had little that the Chinese wanted in exchange for the growing demand for tea, and to pay for it the East India Company began shipping opium to China from their possessions in India. As the tea trade grew, the British government imposed a heavy import duty on tea shipped to its North American colonies, resulting in the 'Boston Tea Party'. By 1834, the East India Company had lost its monopoly of the China tea trade, and five ports – Canton, Amoy, Foochow, Ningpo and Shanghai – were opened for free trade, making new supplies of tea available to British merchants and traders. Two years later, America contracted a similar trading agreement with China, as did France.

Of the four crops obtained from a tea bush in a year, the first two were for export, the other two for domestic use. The first picking, called the first chop, began in the middle of April and was of the smallest but best flavoured and the most valuable tea. The first teas of the season to arrive in London were assured of high prices. The ships carrying them brought wealth to their owners and masters and glory and renown to the ships.

As a tea clipper, *Mimosa*'s sailing capabilities would be tested to the full as she sped from China to the London docks with her cargoes of teas, and safety would be forfeited for speed in the most dangerous seas in the world

Thomas Kemp

Thomas Kemp was born in Liverpool in 1820, the only surviving son of Thomas Kemp, also a seaman, and Mary (née Hinton), both of Liverpool. He had two older sisters, Ann and Ellen, and two younger, Maria Ann and Mary Ann. An older brother, Thomas Tinchett Kemp, died in childhood.

Thomas Kemp went to sea when he was fifteen, possibly as an apprentice. In 1850, when he was thirty, he obtained a First Class rating in his master's Certificate of Competency. He married Sarah Maynard, possibly at the time of *Mimosa*'s construction, or just after receiving his certificate.

Although it was not obligatory by law, until passing of the Merchant Shipping Act of 1854, most owners required that their masters, as well as first and second mates, held certificates of Competency or of Service for Foreign-Going ships. (Ships bound to some place beyond the limits of the River Elbe or Brest.) A Certificate of Service required no written examination and was obtained through serving as master or mate on any British ship for a given number of years. Thomas Kemp represented a new generation of master mariners – young, literate and skilled in the many aspects of commanding a merchant clipper ship.

The examination for the Certificate of Competency was a written one, requiring that the candidates be literate. Before the examination could be taken, candidates had to provide a testimonial of character, sobriety and good conduct on board the ships on which they had served. Candidates had to be at least twenty-one years old and had to have spent a minimum of six years at sea, one year serving as first mate and one as second. They needed to have knowledge of navigation by stars, sun and moon as well as by instruments, to know the nature of tides, to be able to read charts and understand signals. They also had to be cognisant of the law as it pertained to management of a crew and agents on shore, and to know how to prevent scurvy.

Thomas Kemp obtained a First Class rating in his five-hour examination and duly received his Certificate of Competency. He captained two ships (*Creamore*, on the Liverpool to Newfoundland run, and *Lord John Russell*, on the Liverpool to Brazil run) before being given the command of Vining & Killey's newest acquisition.[11]

His skills as a master mariner would be tested to the full on his first voyage to China.

Preparations

Mimosa made four voyages to China, three to Shanghai, for the 1854, 1855 and 1856 tea seasons, under Thomas Kemp, and one to Foochow in 1863, under her third master, Archibald Johnson. Each round voyage took from eleven months to almost a year. Her first voyage to Shanghai, in 1854, was her second voyage under Thomas Kemp. Following her launch, Thomas Kemp had sailed *Mimosa* to Rio de Janeiro from North Shields. He then took her to Buenos Aires, perhaps to load a cargo of hides or tallow. From Buenos Aires, she sailed to Ireland, arriving in Queenstown, in County Cork, on February 26, 1854. She arrived in Bristol on March 11. She then made the run to Liverpool, where Thomas Kemp was informed that he would be sailing her to Shanghai. The voyage to Shanghai would be far more hazardous, longer and more arduous than her voyage to South America, and countless ships had floundered on the uncharted reefs of the China Seas.

Her date of departure from Liverpool would have been advertised, and merchants wishing to send goods to Hong Kong or Shanghai would contact Vining & Killey. No one had more to do with the reputation of a ship than her master. A ship's name was seldom mentioned without her master's; and both would have appeared on all relevant documents and posters.

As *Mimosa* lay in her loading berth, all freshly painted, every rope carefully coiled in its place, her figurehead decorated with bright ribbons, a large poster in her rigging announced the port for which she was destined. Before she could be loaded, the ballast needed to hold her steady in dock, when she was empty, had to be hauled away in horse drawn carts and her hold swept clean. Then, her cargo was loaded, the relevant documents and customs forms completed and her crew hired and signed on.

Voyage to Shanghai

Mimosa must have looked glorious, setting out for her first voyage to China on June 8, 1854, with her acres of sail filling out in the wind as she dropped her pilot beyond Mersey Bar, a glint of her copper sheathing visible as she rose and dipped in the swells. The small crowd of onlookers that lined the wharf would have caught their breaths in wonder at the lines of the new little clipper, flying the Union Jack as well as the flag that identified her ownership; and undoubtedly Robert Vining and William Killey and other part-owners would have been there to witness the departure. On board was a son or brother of Robert Vining – George Vining, possibly as supercargo.[12]

Sarah Kemp, holding the baby born in 1853 – a boy, called Thomas after his father and grandfather – watched *Mimosa*'s departure with mixed emotions. It would be a year before she would see her husband again, assuming that the ship she herself had named and called upon God to protect with all who sailed on her, would not come to grief in the uncharted China seas. Thomas Kemp's widowed mother, who kept a lodging-house, and his sisters would also have been on the wharf to wave him farewell.

A clipper's sea-going life was a decade at most; and *Mimosa*'s best runs were expected to be on her first voyages, when she was at the peak of her seaworthiness. As her owners watched, they would have seen her tiers of studding sails puff out sideways as they caught the wind.

Immediately, the crew were put to work. Some were ordered to trim the sails. Others, whether they had ever been on board a clipper before or not, were ordered to climb aloft and inch out to the ends of the booms, to reef or shake out *Mimosa*'s heavy sails, getting what grip they could on the thin footropes under their bare or slippered heels.

Two months after leaving Liverpool, one of the crew fell overboard when trying to tie a sail during a storm. *Mimosa* was sailing fast in such winds, and there would have been no way to turn her in time to save him, even if they could have seen him, for it was after one o'clock in the morning.

Mimosa followed the conventional route to Shanghai by sailing south to the Bay of Biscay, where she would have encountered the storms prevalent there, past the Azores, Madeira, and the Canary and Cape Verde Islands. Instead of sailing southeast towards the African coast and round the Cape of Good Hope, Thomas Kemp, like all experienced captains, would have avoided the mid-Atlantic, where the area of Doldrums were widest, and hugged the coast of Brazil, where, at the bulge of the Brazilian coastline, the band of calms was at its narrowest. He would then have followed the Great Eastern Route, picking up the winds of the Roaring Forties to speed her into the immensity of the Pacific Ocean against the Northeast Trades to Shanghai, calling first at Hong Kong, to discharge cargo.

There were numerous cases of insubordination and drunkenness among the crew, several of whom were brought before the Marine Magistrate at Hong Kong. Three were sentenced to fourteen days' hard labour, while a fourth was sentenced to a month for attempting to incite a mutiny. The cook, against whom there had been violent complaints of spoiled victuals since leaving Liverpool, was discharged, having refused to continue with his duties on the grounds that two of the crew had been beating him. The first mate was also discharged, forcibly so, since he had been continually drunk and abusive to Kemp throughout the voyage. Upon being released from their two-week prison sentence, two of the crew refused to rejoin the ship and were threatened with eighty-four days imprisonment by the magistrate unless they did so.

With seven new crew men to replace the seven who were discharged, possibly 'shanghaied', drunk or drugged, from taverns, *Mimosa* sailed on to Shanghai.

Shanghai, at the mouth of the great Yangtze-kiang, some four hundred and fifty miles north of Foochow and double that from Hong Kong, was then the centre of European commerce in China. The port was divided into three distinct concessions, each being governed by its own laws. The American concession, closest to the harbour, was the largest, although not as important as the British concession with its wide streets, or as aesthetic as the French concession with its handsome architecture.

Mimosa's sails would have been taken in, the anchor dropped, a pilot boarded, and a tug would have towed her up the mud-coloured Whangpoo River to the anchorage on the British concession, where she would receive her cargo of tea. Everywhere was colour, noise and clamour. Gongs and drums from square-bowed junks or sampans ornamented with dragons and gigantic painted eyes accompanied the setting of the sun every evening, and the water was aglow with the reflections of the tapers placed on every boat. Boys shouted from the wash boats that attached themselves to every vessel. Floating brothels bedecked with flowers rocked seductively on the oil-smooth waves, their shutters closed despite the heat. Stately barges with awnings supported by pillars, their slender white oars dipping into the river, carried customs officials. Strange new smells were wafted on every breeze. Tea factories and warehouses fronted the water, and European agents haggled over tea prices with pigtailed Chinese merchants, in the universally-spoken *pidgin*. Smart, white-painted, American paddle-steamers, tugs, sampans and junks passed up and down on the river, along with other clippers, their crews, perhaps, glancing at the young newcomer anchored at the British concession, her buff-coloured sails not yet bleached white by the sun and sea.

As soon as *Mimosa* was docked and the pilot paid, a Chinese official, followed by a coolie holding an umbrella over his head to protect him from the sun, came aboard to levy customs duties. With a brass rod, he measured *Mimosa*'s length and breadth, multiplied them, added 100% for *cumshaw* (tips) and 50% more for his own fee, while a clerk with an abacus and writing implements recorded the remaining items of cargo.

While *Mimosa* waited for chests of tea to be brought down in sampans from the plantations that lined the river, her hold would have been prepared for the ballast, and heavy booms fixed to ropes were pulled back and forth along the copper bottom, to clear it of barnacles and weed, which would slow her on her homeward voyage.

Being a new clipper, with the highest classification, coming from the same shipyard as the almost legendary *Cairngorm*, Thomas Kemp, or George Vining, if he were acting as supercargo, would have had little trouble in negotiating a cargo at a better freight rate per ton of tea than many of *Mimosa*'s rivals awaiting cargoes. Her size, too, was an advantage, the larger clippers having to wait weeks until a full cargo was taken on, or having to sail half-loaded. As he waited for the tea to be brought from the factories in the hills, where it had been tested, graded and packed into wood chests lined with lead, Thomas Kemp would have arranged for the ballasting to begin.

Tea, being so light a cargo, a ton or more of beach pebbles would have been loaded for ballast by Chinese stevedores. The layer of pebbles would have been smoothed level and rounded up the sides to fit the upward curved contours of the hold, so that the chests would lie in a shallow arch, with a floor of planking placed over them. The whole area would then have been measured meticulously with a brass rod by the Chinese superintending the loading, in order to calculate the number of chests that would fit, and surplus pebbles would have been removed. As an added precaution, Thomas Kemp might have instructed *Mimosa*'s carpenter to build a large box and fill it with anchor chains and iron kentledge, to serve as portable ballast that could be moved about, to keep *Mimosa* in trim as she changed from one tack to another.

After the ballast was laid, sampans bearing the Vining & Killey house flag would have begun bringing the chests of tea. Each lead-lined chest was wrapped in a couple of layers of greased, transparent paper bearing the name of the tea it contained and MIMOSA written clear and large. The loading of tea chests required care and skill. The chests and half-chests were loaded, tier upon tier, and wedged and hammered so tightly into place that they assumed the curved shape of the hold in order to hold them fast, even in the stormiest weather. The inferior tea was placed on the bottom to protect the better teas from risk of damage from the bilge water, since the teas were susceptible to fumes.

Ships loading tea at Shanghai invariably loaded raw silk as well, and bales of raw silk, wrapped in oiled canvas to protect them against the wet, would have been carefully placed between the tiers of tea chests. The trim of a ship being essential to her speed (an inch out of trim would slow her) more pebbles and shingle would have been forced into the spaces between the chests and the curve of the hull. When the loading was finished and the last chest had been hammered into place with a wooden mallet, a covering of split bamboos and canvas would have been laid on top, and the hatches closed and sealed. Finally, other sampans came alongside with the fresh water and provisions *Mimosa* would need for her voyage back to England.

A Race

When two ships left the same port, bound for the same destination, masters laid a wager that their clipper would be first back into port. Ship owners and merchants in Liverpool and London followed the race from port to port with keen monetary interest. There was a bonus for the master who docked in port first, and glory for the ship. All being fair in love and clipper racing, masters resorted to every device in order to attain and keep a lead, from bribing pilots to lead a rival clipper onto a reef, to making a pretence of anchoring at night to induce their rivals to do likewise and, when they had done so, raising their sails and racing away under cover of darkness.

Mimosa left Shanghai on December 21, 1854, loaded with tea and silk. Sailing from Shanghai, two days later, was the 671-ton *Spirit of the North*, also built in 1853. It is likely that a challenge would have been issued and wagers laid between the two masters and between the crews.

There was more at stake than the wager. If *Mimosa* could make the voyage to London in better time than the *Spirit of the North* she would be guaranteed early loading and good freight rates on her next voyage to Shanghai, while slower ships would wait longer, or even in vain, for a cargo.

There were various routes that could be taken to England from China, the choice depending on the time of year and the experience of the ship's master. Thomas Kemp, weighing up the choices for a faster speed, decided to set a course for Anjer, situated in a shallow declivity in the volcanic coastal range west of the fifteen-mile-wide Sunda Strait, between Sumatra and Java.

Hazards abounded on the fifteen-thousand-mile run from Shanghai to the East or West India Docks in London, where cargoes of tea were unloaded. The China Sea was poorly mapped, and ships were constantly wrecked on uncharted reefs. The monsoons, which blew erratically from one point of the compass to another, were another concern. If the summer monsoons were avoided, ships were in danger of encountering the winter ones, and the teas grown around Shanghai could not be harvested before the summer monsoons were at their worst. Then, there were the Chinese and Malay pirates. In the year of *Mimosa*'s first voyage to Shanghai, seven hundred ships in the Hong Kong area alone were plundered by pirates in innocent-looking fishing boats. For that reason, *Mimosa* would have carried a couple of small cannons, and showed no lights during the night; and it is certain that Thomas Kemp was no different from his contemporaries, in pushing *Mimosa* to the limits of her sailing capabilities.

Mimosa reached Anjer, twenty-five hundred miles away, on January 7, having taken only seventeen days to do so, which was the fastest time made by a ship of her size that season.

In the scorching calm, a sudden squall would sweep in from nowhere, accompanied by torrents of rain. The strong currents and monsoon winds of Java or Sumatra often forced ships to drop anchor in frustration several times, before being able to navigate the narrow channel that varied in depth from five hundred feet in mid-channel to twenty feet or less at the edges. Landing being impossible because of the trees that grew so densely at the water's edge, it could take days or even weeks to get through the Sunda Strait. At Anjer, where brightly-coloured birds flew among the groves of tamarind and banyan trees, Thomas Kemp would have paused only long enough to raise flags to signal his position to the Dutch authorities on shore. *Mimosa*'s time would have been conveyed by telegraph at Anjer to Robert Vining's agents in London, where excitement would have been high. On the other side of the Sunda Strait, *Mimosa*'s sails filled out to send her speeding through the emerald-green seas towards Mauritius. The *Spirit of the North* reached Anjer two days later, on January 9, unable to decrease *Mimosa*'s lead.

It was between Anjer and Mauritius, in the Southeast Trades of the Indian Ocean, that clippers made their best times. It was also the most exhilarating part of the passage. If Thomas Kemp was celebrating, he was celebrating too soon, however. In the Indian Ocean, the Doldrums slowed *Mimosa*'s progress, most likely for a week, until she caught the Southeast Trade winds, which sent her round the Cape of Good Hope and speeding northwards. She passed St Helena, where she replenished her supply of fresh water and provisions, and passed into the calms of the

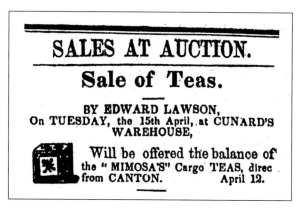

Advertisement for the auction of Mimosa's *tea.*

Equator and the Horse Latitudes – so called because, when ships were becalmed there, their cargos of horses were sometimes driven overboard in order to conserve the stores of water.

Instead of sailing eastwards across the North Atlantic towards England, however, *Mimosa* sailed north to Halifax, Nova Scotia. She arrived in Halifax in April, and one of the young apprentices deserted. On April 15, 1856, her cargo of tea was auctioned at Cunard's Warehouse.[13] It is not known if Halifax was a scheduled destination.

Mimosa arrived in George's Basin in Liverpool on May 10, 1854. Her voyage to China had taken eleven months. The *Spirit of the North* arrived in London on April 15, taking 113 days for the voyage from Shanghai.

Second and Third Voyages to Shanghai

By the beginning of June, less than a month after her return to Liverpool, *Mimosa* sailed again to Shanghai, and returned on January 13, 1856.

A month later, on February 19, *Mimosa* sailed again for Shanghai, under Thomas Kemp, leaving Shanghai on September 22, 1856, where some of the crew who had signed on in Liverpool deserted. Another of Robert Vining's ships, *Reindeer*, was lost at sea, possibly wrecked, and expectations that *Mimosa*'s third voyage to China would help recoup his losses were high.

Mimosa would have had to sail fast in order to avoid the northeast monsoon that begins early in October in the northern part of the China Sea, and which reaches the southern part in November. *Mimosa* made good time, however, perhaps taking advantage of the brisker winds, for she reached Anjer on October 25, well ahead of the seasonal squalls and typhoons.

She sailed up the coast of Africa, through the Azores, into the Bay of Biscay and on to the English Channel. She passed the Isle of Wight and, by nightfall, she would have seen Beachy Head and the Dungeness Lighthouse, where she signalled for a pilot to come aboard and guide her into the Thames estuary.

On January 18, 1857, she reached London, having taken118 days for the journey from Shanghai, making as good a time as the other clippers of her size on the Shanghai to London run that year.

Arrival in Port

When a ship was sighted in the Channel, owners were notified by telegraph. Weathervanes erected above their offices and geared to compass clocks inside their boardrooms gave them an indication of the prevailing wind and whether their investment would dock in good time.

By the time *Mimosa* reached the gates of the East India Docks, the brokers acting for various consignees were down at the docks, ready to break open a few chests, from which samples of teas were taken, to assess their quality and freshness. These were sent to dealers in Mincing Lane, who auctioned them to wholesalers. The dock gates were slammed shut and locked, the crew discharged. Alone, *Mimosa* rocked at her mooring, waiting to unload. As soon as the tea was unloaded, it was stored in a dock warehouse, to be dispatched to Hamburg, Rotterdam, Barcelona, St Petersburg or Helsinki.

Almost a month later, on February 10, she sailed to Liverpool for her next voyage and arrived exactly one week later. Robert Vining and William Killey met with Thomas Kemp to determine what repairs needed to be carried out. The next voyage was planned, outward-going cargo sought, customs formalities completed and a new crew signed on.

Mimosa's next voyage was to Brazil, to load sugar. It was her last voyage under Thomas Kemp.

Foochow

Mimosa's last voyage to China was to Foochow, on March 26, 1863; her master was forty-nine-year-old Archibald Johnson, from Liverpool, an experienced seaman, but illiterate. He could sign his name, but the log entries are not written in his handwriting.

Mimosa first anchored at Shanghai, having passed uneventfully through Anjer on September 15, where the carpenter, who had listed *Mimosa* as his previous ship, died of cholera.

Mimosa remained for more than a month at Shanghai, where, on Saturday, September 12, two seamen, one from Marseilles and the other from Bordeaux, deserted. The entry in the log states simply that they ran away.

In the six years since *Mimosa*'s previous voyage to China, Foochow had replaced Canton and Shanghai to become the principle tea port in China. The tea picked in the surrounding province of Fukien, where the best quality black teas were grown, was ready to be harvested in May and June, a good two months earlier than anywhere else in China, enabling ships to get away well before the south-west monsoons, which buffet the China Seas throughout July and August.

Foochow lies twenty-five miles upriver on the Min, which twists tortuously through terraced plantations and villages, between steep gorges that are so narrow that monkeys leaping from one side to the other often got their tails entangled in clippers' rigging. Hill upon hill rises on either side, their peaks blurring into the distance. *Chow-chow* currents and the sluicing of waters encountered around each tortuous bend threatened to wreck *Mimosa* against the rocks, as a pilot – either Chinese or one of the many Europeans addicted to alcohol and opium, for whom any other sort of life was no longer an option – guided her to the Pagoda Anchorage, where sampans brought down the teas from the plantations that lined the river.

The Pagoda Anchorage, where the Min widens to some two miles in places, giving the river the appearance of an inland lake ringed by mountains rising steeply from the water, was the loveliest of anchorages and the most dangerous to reach. An old pagoda on an island cliff top gave the anchorage its name. According to legend, it had been built by the beautiful wife of a young sea captain, so that she might watch for his return from a long sea voyage. Returning after years voyaging and seeing the unfamiliar sight of a pagoda, he thought that he had come to the wrong place, and sailed away again, leaving his wife to throw herself into the sea in grief.

By December 5, *Mimosa* was loading tea for London, after which, she was towed back downriver. So fast was the river that it could have taken as many as twenty boats tied to her sides to tow her to where the river widened at the sea. Although she took only ten days to reach Anjer from Foochow, she took 121 more to reach London on March 3, 1864, making a stop at St Helena, perhaps for repairs, making 131 days in total.

It was her last voyage to China.

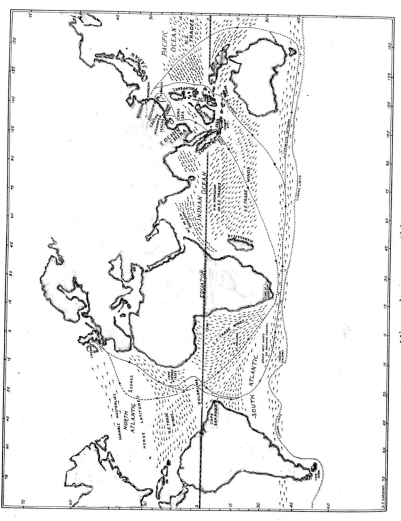

Mimosa's routes to China.

Part IV

The Sweetest Cargo

Here, sheltered from every wind and surrounded by a country exuberantly rich, fleets may ride at anchor in a gulf which seems as if formed by nature to be the emporium of the world and receive its shipping, while the town itself, seen picturesquely crowning the high bluff that circles round the eastern side of the bay, appears a fitting mistress of the lovely scene.

William Scully, *Brazil: its Provinces and Chief Cities.*

Sugar

Sugar cane, *saccharum officinarum*, is a tall, perennial, grass-like plant with numerous erect stems, from six to twelve feet in length, which, in their upper portions, bear long, narrow leaves. It is propagated by cuttings: a piece of stem bearing buds at its nodes will root rapidly when placed in the ground. Its native country is unknown; but it is thought to have originated in Northern India, where allusions to the sweet sap of a honey-bearing reed that produced a granulated, sand-like product, known as *shakkara,* appear in Sanskrit literature from around 1400 BC.

The art of boiling the cane to make dense syrup was carried to China in the first half of the 7th century, where the use of ashes to produce crystals was learned from Egyptian traders. *Shakkara* was known to Arab physicians, who listed it in their pharmacopoeia as an additive to bitter-tasting herbs and potions, to make them more palatable. Sugar cane was introduced by the Arabs into Persia, Morocco, Syria, Palestine, Cyprus, Crete, Sicily, the south of Spain and Madeira. The Crusaders discovered the sweet-tasting reed called *zucra* and took it back with them to France, where the crystals derived from its juice were used in medical formulae and were extremely costly.

In the Middle Ages, Venice was the European centre of the sugar trade, controlling distribution throughout the then known world, where it was sold raw. (Sugar was not referred to as white until 1430, which indicates that purification techniques were in use by then.) Sugars – dark brown and moulded into cones or blocks – were referred to as being 'of' the place in which they were grown: Syria, Palestine, the Dodecanese, Cyprus, Alexandria, Babylon, Barbary, Crete, Morocco, etc. 'Sugre' first appeared in English in 1299, in a record of a shipment sent to London in 1319 by one Tomasso Loredano, a merchant of Venice, in exchange for wool.

In the age of discovery, the cultivation of sugar was dominated by the Portuguese and Spanish. In 1420, Dom Enrique, Infante of Portugal, known as the Navigator, transported it from Cyprus and Sicily to Madeira, from where it was exported to England, Florence and Germany, primarily for medical use, through Venetian channels.

On his second voyage to the New World, in 1493, Columbus introduced sugar cane to the island of Hispaniola, now known as Haiti, and, in 1515, cane was taken from Hispaniola to Puerto Rico and, five years after that, to Mexico. The first commercial production of sugar in the New World was undertaken in 1550, when the Portuguese built *engenhos* (mills) near Pernambuco, in Northeast Brazil. By 1526, the Portuguese were shipping sugar to Lisbon from Pernambuco, which became the principal source of sugar for Europe for the next two centuries.

By the Elizabethan and Jacobean Ages, sugared almonds, sugar meats, sugar pellets, and flowers modelled with delicate ivory tools, even plates, platters, cups and bowls made of sugar paste and coloured with crushed violet, cowslip, gillyflower or rose petals and flavoured with cinnamon or ginger, which could be consumed after the meal was over, began to appear at banquet tables. Edible tableware – light in weight and elegantly white or delicately hued – was a sign of wealth. It was not until Chinese porcelain came to be imported with the cargoes of tea that anything resembling it replaced the heavy, dark-glazed earthenware pottery or Dutch delft.

By the 16th century, refined sugar was replacing honey as a sweetener. By the middle of the 17th century, the Brazilian sugar industry had begun to expand rapidly. The Dutch East India Company seized Pernambuco from the Portuguese, and, by 1640, Pernambuco was the world's largest exporter of sugar to Amsterdam.

With larger quantities available from Madeira and their Brazilian possessions in Bahia, the Dutch purchased crude sugar in Lisbon, by-passing the traditional Venetian channels, refined it in Antwerp and Amsterdam and distributed it all over Europe, where it continued to be a costly luxury and exotic condiment, seen only on the tables of the wealthy, at weddings and festive occasions, or used medicinally. The variety of cane taken to the Spanish and Portuguese colonies in the New World from Spain and Madeira was known as Creole. The species introduced to Mauritius from Tahiti was known as Bourbon. Bourbon cane, in turn, was taken from Mauritius to the French West Indies around 1780, and became the principal variety of cane grown throughout the Caribbean.

Molasses, the thick, syrupy, uncrystalized portion of the cane juice, was imported in 12 cwt. puncheons and barrels. A coarse sugar, called bastards, was extracted from it, the residue of which was termed treacle. White sugar was made from *moscovado* that had been boiled and clarified with charcoal, blood or lime, and poured into conical-shaped moulds. The resulting cones and loaves, wrapped in white paper with an additional covering of blue, were packed in casks for delivery to grocers from the sugar houses in London and Liverpool.

During the 1850s, more than half Europe's sugar came from Pernambuco and Bahia, and the centre of the European market had shifted to London, where grades like London Raw and First Brown categorized it by colour and purity.

Bahia

South, below the huge bulge of Brazil, nestles the island-studded Baía de Todos os Santos, where, once, a thousand ships lay at anchor in any one month, waiting to load barrels of unrefined sugar. Of the hundred or more islands in the lapis lazuli-blue waters of the bay, some are ninety miles or more in length, while others are mere specks of land. Countless creeks, coves and inlets indent the coastline of the bay, into which numerous rivers and streams empty their waters. Extending back from the shoreline is a gently undulating landscape of rounded hills and low *serras*, where erosion along the many rivers has made rugged bluffs.

In 1500, Pedro Alvares Cabral, driven off course by adverse winds on his voyage to the East, reached the coast of an enormous, forest-covered land, and sent a small vessel to Lisbon, to announce his discovery, which he named Vera Cruz (True Cross), subsequently known as Santa Cruz (Holy Cross), before proceeding on to India. Amerigo Vespucci was dispatched from Portugal, to explore the latest acquisition to the Crown. The navigator's first voyage was unsuccessful, but, on the second, he discovered a bay of such heavenly natural beauty that he named it Baía de Todos os Santos — the Bay of all Saints.

Initially, the new acquisition appeared to offer no wealth to rival that of Portugal's colonies in Africa and India, or even Madeira, the Azores or the Cape Verde Islands, and was of little interest to Portugal. To the north was a huge river with numberless tributaries, flowing through vast, impenetrable forests, and to the south and centre, a three-thousand-foot escarpment presented a formidable barrier; and the northeast was a drought-stricken stony desert. For the first two centuries of colonial rule, there was almost no communication between one region and another. Travel by land (and in such a land) was well nigh impossible, and it was easier to sail to Europe than it was to travel from the arid northeast *sertâo* to the hinterlands of the south. Only the narrow coastal plain, extending landward from the shoreline of the Bay of All Saints, offered an accessible foothold; but it had little to offer except brazilwood (*pau brasil*) and stunningly beautiful natural anchorages.

In the 17th century the colony was so large that it was divided into two administrations, each being governed separately, which led to the formation of two Brazils or, simply, the Brazils.

The commerce in brazilwood was never large – only from three to five shipments a year – despite the fact that, in sixteenth-century Europe, the red dye extracted from it was in great demand for the dyeing of textiles. It was, however, the first of the economic booms that gave the land its enduring name. Licences to trade were granted to Portuguese merchants, who could not afford the longer and more costly voyages to India, and to Portuguese Jews, who were prohibited from entering the more lucrative trade of the Orient.

Where one goes others follow. Less than three decades after its discovery, the French and the Dutch were exploring the coast and establishing settlements, and merchants from other European countries were obtaining licences to trade in brazilwood. With a population of little more than a million, Portugal could not colonize Brazil as it had Goa and

Macao, Madeira, the Azores and its African colonies. It was clear that the Treaty of Tordesillas, by which, in 1494, the entire non-Christian world had been arbitrarily divided between Spain and Portugal by Papal sanction, would not protect Brazil from other powers that looked westwards across the Atlantic.

Following the system that had proved successful in Madeira and the Azores a century before, the huge landmass of Brazil was divided into fifteen *capitanías*, each of which was a separate colony, directly subordinate to Portugal. With the *capitanía* system established, the Crown began parcelling out vast grants of land – *sesmarias* – to those held in favour by the emperor, whereby Brazil became the first European colony in America to be founded upon agriculture, as opposed to the acquisition of precious metals. Some of the *sesmarias* were the size of European countries; others, such as the ones around Bahia, were on a comparatively smaller scale.

For three centuries, Bahia was the colony's economic heartland. While Sao Paulo was an obscure settlement of struggling subsistence farmers, and Rio de Janeiro was a wretched town with a bad reputation for yellow fever, Bahia was the jewel and glory of the Portuguese empire. Salvador da Bahia, established on a high bluff overlooking the Bay of All Saints, referred to simply as Bahia, even on official documents, was for two centuries the capital of Brazil and second only to Lisbon in grandeur and importance. The source of its great wealth was sugar, introduced from Madeira in the 1530s, which was planted along the narrow strip of coast extending from Salvador da Bahia northwards to Pernambuco.

For over two centuries, Bahia, together with Pernambuco, had what amounted to the world monopoly on sugar, which yielded more revenue to the Portuguese Crown than the trade with India, with all its silks and rubies. Native Indian labour was used to clear the trees, burn off the undergrowth and stumps and to plant and cut the canes. When, after a few decades, disease or warfare had reduced their population, African slaves were imported in increasing numbers from the Portuguese-controlled slave-trading ports on the west coast of Africa.

By the 17th century, many of the refining processes were in the hands of the Dutch, who plundered the sugar-laden Portuguese ships and eventually tried to seize the sugar-rich states for themselves. In 1624, they succeeded in capturing Salvador da Bahia, which they held for only a few months. When they were driven out of their foothold in Bahia, they went northward and captured Pernambuco. For over twenty years, from 1632 to 1654, they held the entire Brazilian coast, from northern Bahia to the mouth of the Amazon. Up to two-thirds of the sugar that entered Europe through refineries in the Netherlands was carried by Dutch ships from Brazil. When the Dutch were finally forced to abandon their Brazilian conquests, they took their knowledge of sugar production acquired in Brazil to the Caribbean. They established plantations in Barbados; and sugar was soon being produced in other Dutch as well as French and English plantations in the West Indies. By the end of the 17th century, the sugar industry in Brazil, although still vast, no longer had a world monopoly; sugar from the Caribbean dominated the European market. The boom, which lasted for over two centuries, was over.

Britain and Brazil

The sugar industry in Brazil did not abruptly vanish in 1650, when its spectacular boom ended. By the early 19th century, sugar exports began to increase, new mills were built, and, by 1850, Brazil was the world's third largest producer.

By 1853, when *Mimosa* was constructed, with the lucrative Brazilian trade in mind, Brazil was riding the crest of a wave of economic expansion under Dom Pedro II, who was just five years into his reign. Dom Pedro wanted to modernize his empire, and it was capital and expertise from Britain, more than from any other foreign nation, that was providing the commercial infrastructure and necessary investments. The need for British ships to carry all that the viceregal capital of Rio de Janeiro required, and carry all that Brazil could harvest back to London and Liverpool, had never been greater and would increase in the decade ahead. The first telegraph line, built and maintained by British engineers, linked Rio de Janeiro to the provinces and beyond. The first railroad was inaugurated, and British mail packets provided regular services across the Atlantic.

Even before the unhappy Catherine of Braganza was married to Charles II, alliances between England and Portugal had been forged. In 1147, English crusaders helped the young King Afonso of Burgundy to capture Lisbon from the Moors, and successive treaties cemented the alliance. In later centuries, as Portugal carved out a maritime empire that was then far in advance of England's, England was given commercial privileges in return for guarantees of military support, should Portugal be threatened by Spain or Holland. Reciprocal treaties further guaranteed liberties to each to trade in the territories of the other that greatly favoured English merchants. There was no law limiting maritime trade, and even after the Cromwellian Navigation Laws came into effect and remained law long after the man who had instigated them was dead, goods destined for England could be carried from the East Indies, West Africa, Macao and the Brazils to Portuguese ports on Portuguese ships, and be imported to their final destination on any of the English ships anchored in Oporto, Vigo or Lisbon itself. On the marriage of Charles II to Catherine of Braganza, England was given Bombay as a permanent trading post, together with the privilege of establishing merchant houses in Bahia, Pernambuco and Rio de Janeiro, as well as in the West Indies.

Lisbon lay on the route between England and the British colonies in America, and a free trade was carried on between Britain's American colonies and Madeira. Brandies, wines (especially Madeira), salt and spices were traded for fish and lumber from Newfoundland. Woollen clothing, and tapestries and carpets were in high demand in Portugal where, increasingly, English merchants and artisans were settling.

Over time, Portugal became the warehouse for the English merchandise destined for the Portuguese colonies, much of it carried on British ships. Whatever Portugal needed, England supplied, both in military support against the Dutch and the Spanish and in goods to sustain their shaky colonial power. The balance of trade tipped strongly in Britain's favour, making Portugal its virtual commercial vassal.

In 1808, Napoleon's armies invaded Portugal. The court and royal family and all the machinery of government, with the royal treasury, fled to Brazil under the protection of a large British naval escort, becoming the only European monarchs to rule an empire from one of its colonies. Industrially, Brazil was a backward country in a backward continent. There were no printing presses, no universities, few roads and no railways. There were no manufacturing industries, no building materials, coal or textiles. The royal administration needed new sources of revenue to support itself in exile. Emperor Dom Joao opened all Brazilian ports to international trade and favoured British merchants over those of any other nation. Treaties to trade with Portugal were extended to trade in the vast colony of virtually untapped resources. Import duties imposed on British goods were less than on those from Portugal, and considerably less than on goods imported from any other country. Brazil bought more from Britain than it sold. Despite the vast supplies of sugar, cotton and, later, coffee shipped to London or Liverpool on British ships, the Brazilian debt mounted. Brazil's economic dependency on Britain was complete and lasted for over a century.

Under the royal residency, Brazil felt the stirrings of nationhood. Printing presses began to operate, newspapers were published. Rio de Janeiro blossomed into a viceregal city; and the magnificence of its new buildings was matched only by the beauty of their setting. When Brazil declared its independence from Portugal in 1822, Britain recognized the new nation, in exchange for a transfer of the same commercial privileges enjoyed with Portugal.

Britain demanded, too, that Brazil abolish its slave trade. Brazil refused to do this, despite a treaty agreeing to the end of slave traffic, since its economy depended on it, and slavery was not abolished until the second half of the 19th century. British ships patrolled the seas to intercept Brazil-bound slavers, whose crews threw their cargo overboard in order to evade detection. However, abolition of the Brazilian slave trade would, and eventually did, impede Brazil's output of sugar, to the advantage of Britain's sugar trade with the West Indies, and many freed male slaves were pressed into service on British men-of-war and merchant vessels needing crews. Such was the animosity against Britain over the matter of slavery that British ships and their masters and crews were frequently targets of hostility and violent attacks in Brazilian ports.

Despite the thorny issue of slavery, Brazil imposed no restrictions on British trade, and conceded to Britain the right to appoint her own judges in Brazilian ports. Until the end of the 19th century, Britain exported more to Brazil than to the rest of South America and Mexico combined.

British foods were a staple of every Brazilian of means – Cheshire cheeses, Huntley and Palmers' biscuits, Jersey potatoes, Bass beer, English butter for white bread made from English flour. Furniture, sinks, washstands, bathtubs and even pipes and plumbing were imported from England. Every *farmacia ingleza* stocked English toothpowder, soap, and eau de cologne and lavender water. Men (and sometimes women) smoked cigars manufactured in England, wrote their letters on English writing paper, with English ink, and were buried in English coffins. Wars and revolutions were carried on with English weapons and firearms. Hats, canes, umbrellas and parasols came from England, and no Brazilian *senhor* considered he was well-dressed unless he was attired in an English suit – preferably cut by a London tailor – and wearing Clarks' shoes. Railways, when they came into being, were built and maintained by British engineers. Machinery made from British iron and steel ran on British coal.

Dominated by a plantation society based on slave labour, Brazil manufactured no goods until the second half of the 19th century. With British ships bringing in everything that the factories and textile mills in Britain produced – even the cotton sugar sacks – there was no need. All could be paid for with sugar, cotton or coffee.

Pernambuco

Many of the British commercial interests in the northeast were centred in Pernambuco, the leading sugar exporting centre in Brazil. The wealth of Pernambuco's upper classes matched and even surpassed that of Bahia's. (In the reign of Elizabeth I, 'Fernambuck' was the most flourishing place on the coast of Brazil, with three thousand houses and more than seventy sugar mills in its vicinity, while Bahia had just forty.) Known as the Virginia of Brazil, Pernambuco produced many of the country's statesmen, writers and intellectuals. It also had the highest rate of venereal disease in all Brazil.

As in Bahia, British banks had branches there before any bank was established in Rio de Janeiro. There was a British consul, a British hospital and an Anglican church. The most important export houses in Pernambuco were British. British merchants formed the top echelon of the business hierarchy, followed by British diplomats, engineers and clerks.

Frederick Youle, a former partner of one of *Mimosa*'s shareholders, George Deane, and a shareholder in Robert Vining's *Bonita*, had a large import-export business in Pernambuco. He was a man of importance, for his brother was involved in investments to build one of the first docks and the Sao Paulo railway, the most profitable British railway enterprise in South America. He had a residence in London, and, like most of the British merchants and traders residing in Pernambuco, he undoubtedly sought a partnership with men in the Liverpool shipping business. Frederick Youle was a friend of Joaquim Nabuco, one of Pernambuco's elite, who, strongly influenced by English liberalism, which denied commercial self-interest, became president of the Brazilian Anti-Slavery Society, and was Brazil's first ambassador to the United States, in 1905.

Before 1870, there were few railroads and virtually no roads on which to transport the sugar from the mills in the interior to the ports. Sugar from the mills alongside rivers was transported by 25-ton sail boats, or *jangadas*, made of tree trunks lashed together to form rafts. In areas without access to rivers, caravans of mules, carrying sugar chests and casks of molasses, struggled up or down steep clay hills, along rutted tracks, scoured deeper with every rainfall, and through flat lowlands of mile-wide swamps and mud holes, to the port.

In Pernambuco, the problems of transportation to waiting ships were compounded. The port of Pernambuco, as Recife was formerly called, sometimes referred to as the Venice of South America, is built partly on an island in a lagoon formed by the uniting of two rivers, the Beberibe and the Capabaribe, and partly on the mainland west of the river channels, over which numerous bridges are built. Sao José do Recife, on a sandy peninsula at the outlet of the united rivers, is the oldest part of the seaport and the place where the shipping offices, custom house, merchants' exchange and consulates stood.

A long reef, marked by an old Dutch fort, with a lighthouse at its northern extremity, separates an inner harbour from an outer harbour at Pernambuco and the sugar-loading ports along the coast. It is not a coral reef, but an ancient, sandy breakwater that has consolidated to rock. While the reef shelters the harbour, providing a natural anchorage, a bar across the entrance made it impossible for ships to enter the dock, even at high tide, so that unloading or loading cargo by rowboat or raft was costly and slow.

Brazilian Voyages

Mimosa made nineteen voyages to Brazil – eleven before her voyage to Patagonia and eight afterwards. Each round voyage took between five and seven months, with six weeks to two months at home ports between the end of one voyage and the beginning of the next.

On the second of her Brazilian voyages, she sailed, under Thomas Kemp, to Rio de Janeiro, carrying cargo loaded at Liverpool, and then sailed across the Indian Ocean to Mauritius, where she loaded 8,079 bags of sugar. On his last voyage with her, in May 1857, Thomas Kemp loaded 7,626 bags of sugar in Mauritius, after discharging a cargo at Rio de Janeiro.

In 1857, when *Mimosa* was four years old, Thomas Kemp was given command of Vining & Killey's *Barracouta*, also on the Liverpool to Brazil run, and for her next six voyages, *Mimosa* was under the command of a very different kind of master.

Trevanion Hugo was thirty-three, when he was given command of *Mimosa*, two months after her last voyage with Thomas Kemp. There is no record of him in *Lloyd's Captains' Registers*, and it is possible that *Mimosa* was his first and only ship. He is listed as Comptroller, in charge of accounts, in *Mimosa*'s certificate of registry, and, in 1860, he purchased shares in her. He drove both his crew and *Mimosa* hard, and he believed the worst of the men under his authority, instead of the best. He was intolerant of any infraction of discipline, real or perceived, for which he exacted the full penalty permitted under the Board of Trade laws.

Trevanion Hugo was also short-tempered and possibly a bully. When discharging cargo at Rio de Janeiro, he saw that a young seaman, Alfred Mills, was 'idleing away his time' aloft. Mills 'was spoke to by me, the Master, to get on with his work.' On receiving 'some saucy answer', Hugo resorted to violence, and a fist fight ensued. He noted with evident satisfaction that 'Mills getting the worst of it returned to his work as before a much better man'. On another voyage, a man refused to climb aloft in a gale. Hugo 'gave him a push … and he was put on his back. He went on with his duty very well after that'.

On his first voyage, two of the crew contracted yellow fever in Rio de Janeiro, and died in hospital ashore. Two others were put in jail by the Brazilian authorities in Paraíba for being drunk and disorderly. Another died of heart disease at Mauritius and was buried at sea. There were further incidents of drunkenness, both on sea and ashore. Crews employed as seaman were unable to steer. Stewards refused to serve and clear away meals, or were too intoxicated to do so. Cooks had no skills in cooking and were filthy in their habits.

Under Trevanion Hugo, *Mimosa* made six voyages to Brazil, usually sailing from Rio de Janeiro to Mauritius, again to load sugar. On some voyages, he sailed her northwards to Pernambuco and Maceió, loading sugar and cotton. On May 25, 1860, he purchased 4/64ths shares in her. In September of the same year, he intended to sail *Mimosa* round Cape Horn, possibly to Valparaiso or Iquitos. Fortunately, he changed his mind and sailed her instead to Mauritius, to collect a cargo of sugar. She was not built for the raging storms of the Horn, and it is doubtful whether she would have survived such a voyage.

At the beginning of 1863, his health was evidently of sufficient concern to Vining & Killey that he was divested of his command. Trevanion Hugo, aged thirty-nine, died in December 1864.

Reclassification

On March 18, 1863, *Mimosa* was reclassified from ship to barque, and endorsed in her register accordingly. (A 'bark', originally a term for a nondescript vessel that did not fit other categories, referred to a vessel with three, or sometimes four, masts, with a particular type of rigging.)

Reclassification involved an exhaustive and expensive survey to assess the repairs required, for which she was placed on a dry (graving) dock, or placed on blocks, so that her keel could be examined. Her copper sheathing would have been stripped and some of her planking removed, so that the timbers of her frame could be examined. Alternate treenails were driven out to assess the state of their holes, and the condition of her oakum and caulking checked. Her rigging would have been altered for the modification in sail plan, resulting in a reduction in speed. With her modified rigging, she now required smaller – and therefore cheaper – crews than she had as a full-rigged ship.

Trevanion Hugo was replaced by Archibald Johnson, who made two voyages with her – one to Brazil and the other to Foochow. When *Mimosa* returned from her only voyage to Foochow, on March 11, 1864 – the last of her China voyages – the crewmen received their discharge at the port of London, indicating that her next voyage would commence from there rather than Liverpool. Archibald Johnson is listed as remaining as master, but for whatever reason, he did not sail with her again. For *Mimosa*'s next voyage, Vining & Killey replaced him with George Pepperell, a young man from Devon, who would remain master for her next nine voyages, with whom her name would be forever linked.

On April 21, 1864, *Mimosa* left the Thames under her new master. She was George Pepperell's second ship.

She arrived in Rio de Janeiro almost two months later, on June 16 of the same year. She remained there for over a month; on July 22, departing for Maceió, a cotton port north of Pernambuco.

Mimosa arrived back in London on December 6, 1864; on December 11, she sailed from Liverpool, again to Brazil, and arrived back in Liverpool on April 5, 1865, to await orders for her next voyage. It was to be her most memorable voyage of all.

The Beckoning of Destiny

By 1865, *Mimosa* was twelve years old and well past her sailing prime. Storms, racing and the wear and tear of over a decade at sea had taken their toll. By her second voyage, some replacements of masts and gear, as well as repairs, might have been required. By her fifth, she would have required new sails. Her sheathing would have resembled a patch-work of green copper plates in varying degrees of erosion. She was decidedly dilapidated and looked more like a pauper of the seas than a princess. *Mimosa* had passed her 10-year life expectancy and had survived many of her contemporaries, who had come to grief on the high seas.

But *Mimosa*'s seagoing life had not ended. Her most memorable voyage lay ahead of her. A group of Welshmen were in desperate need of a ship to transport over one hundred men, women and children to Patagonia as the ship originally chartered for the purpose, the *Halton Castle* of the Blythe Line, was still at sea at the scheduled time of departure. The organizers were unable to obtain a ship from the Black Ball Line, since one of the line's associates, Captain Thomas Williams, who himself was

Welsh, refused to transport any of his countrymen, especially women and children, or risk any of the Black Ball Line ships by sailing to a place where so few ships had navigated and where none had ever settled. Robert Vining and William Killey had no such reservations. Business was business, and if some Welshmen were foolhardy enough to want to sail to such an outlandish place as Patagonia, they would be only to happy to provide a ship – one that did not matter too much, of course. And they had just the one that would do.

Part V

Voyage to Patagonia

Patagonia more than answered the descriptions of geographers — bleak, barren, desolate beyond description or conception ... The soil is of a light sandy character and bears nothing worthy of the name of a tree. Low bushes or underwood are tolerably abundant and in the valleys a coarse, wiry grass grows abundantly. Streams of water are rare.

Benjamin Franklin Bourne, *The Captive in Patagonia*

Patagonia

Patagonia, at the most southern part of South America, measures some thirty thousand square miles. One thousand miles long and three hundred and fifty broad at its widest part, it encompasses a fourth of the territory of Argentina and a portion of southern Chile. Bounded by the Andes in the west and by the Atlantic in the east, for centuries it remained isolated and empty, except for nomadic tribes of Araucanian, Tehuelche and Puelche Indians, who hunted the ostrich and the guanaco. Mostly, it was uncharted and unexplored and was a land of almost total mystery.

The northeastern part of Patagonia is an arid desert of thorn and scrub. The moisture-laden winds blowing off the Pacific, forced to rise by the height of the Andes, discharge most of their moisture on the western slopes of the mountains, leaving the winds that blow across the land mass with great violence desiccated. Because of the small amount of moisture in the atmosphere, the temperature falls abruptly after sunset. Dew is unknown in the area. In the winter, the nights are cold, again because of the small amount of heat-retaining moisture in the atmopshere.

Patagonia was discovered in 1520, by Magellan, who, searching for a passage to the Pacific, passed through the straits dividing the island of Tierra del Fuego from the mainland to which he gave his name. Encountering Indians in the region, whose feet were made large by the animal skins they tied around them to protect them from the cold, the smaller Spaniards called them *patagones* (big feet). Ever optimistic of finding another land of mineral wealth, the Spanish Crown sent Simón de Alcazaba to the region in 1534, to try to find it and, when he failed, dispatched Francisco de Camargo, in 1539, with a party of a hundred and fifty men. Of de Camargo's expedition nothing is known. The men vanished without trace, which fuelled rumours of an enchanted city that came to be known as Trapalanda, or the City of the Caesars. Seventy-seven years after Magellan's voyage, Sir Richard Hawkins, with eyes alert for areas of possible commercial interest, explored the coast and decided that there was nothing there. Two centuries later, in 1740, Commodore George Anson, during his voyage in search of new commercial horizons, came to the same conclusion, as did Lord John Byron, who, in 1778, saw the same unchanged scenery. It was visited by Charles Darwin on his voyage on the *Beagle*; by French and Dutch adventurers; by whale- and seal-hunters; and by Jesuit missionaries in the 17th century, and was universally described as an arid wasteland, unfit for human habitation.

Carmen de Patagones in the province of Rio Negro, which bordered on Patagonia to the north, was the extent of any settlement. The dry pampas, from the Rio Negro to Patagonia, was inaccessible except along routes known only to Indians. No settlement of any kind lay between it and Cape Horn; and ships rounding the Horn steered well away from the land.

Four hundred miles south of Carmen de Patagones, along the Atlantic coast, a semicircle of land some twenty feet in length and eight in width forms a natural harbour in a sea that abounds with seals, walruses, whales and penguins. It is called Golfo Nuevo, or New Bay. Here, cliffs rise from the beach to two hundred feet, and stretch away in elevated, arid plains that are, for the most part, covered with thorny, low bushes, which blossom briefly in spring: the *malaspina, duraznillo, calafate, barba de chivo, quilimbay,* and straw-coloured coarse grass, which grow in tough, desiccated tufts. In a good year, the land receives ten inches of rain, and in some years it does not rain at all. The water below ground level is saline and unfit to drink. A wind, oven-hot and dust-laden in summer, ice-sharp in winter, blows almost continuously.

Forty miles south of New Bay, the River Chupat, called Camwy in Welsh, Tswiba in Tehuelche, and which later came to be known universally as the Chubut, empties into the sea, running parallel to the beach for some distance before doing so. The narrow strip of land between the river and the shore conceals its outlet from observation from the sea, and a dangerous sandbar across the mouth of the river makes landing there difficult. The presence of reefs in the estuary is also a source of danger; and the river is subject to periodic flooding.

The Chubut valley stretches inland for forty miles from the river mouth, and is surrounded on both sides of the river by hills. There are no large, indigenous trees; the willow – the *salix humbotiana* – grows along the banks. In some places, the soil is sandy, due to periodic flooding of the river; in others, it is dark-coloured and fertile. The area abounds in wild life: the guanaco, wild cat, fox, armadillo, the South American ostrich or rhea, and the *mara* or Patagonian hare. In the absence of grass, the wild animals graze on the leaves of edible shrubs, which grow in abundance. At the upper termination of the valley, huge rocks stretch along the river for a distance of sixty miles, beyond which are other narrow valleys.

From time to time, small settlements had been established along the Atlantic coast of northern Patagonia, but each attempt had ended in failure, due to the harshness of the climate and terrain and the scarcity of rain. Giving testament to this, an old fort, built on a southward curving spit of land on the north shore of the river, some four miles from its mouth as a protection against the Indians, was occupied for a few brief months before being abandoned. The herds of wild cattle the hunters had sought had long been driven from the area by the Indians, and there seemed little there that was worth remaining for.

The place where the fort was built was to become the capital of the future province of Chubut, which is called Rawson, first known by the Welsh as *Caer Antur* – the Fort of the Venture.

Michael Daniel Jones

The founding father of the Welsh settlement in Patagonia, Michael Daniel Jones, was born on March 2, 1822 in Llanuwchllyn, North Wales; he was the third of five children. Welsh was his first language – his mother and his father tongue. It was the language spoken at table, the language of his prayers at night, and the language of the Bible by which he learned to read. Chapel was not an eleven o'clock Sunday morning obligation. It was a way of life and a way of thought, a social and a religious centre, a place where grievances could be voiced, and its religious leaders wielded a powerful influence over their congregations.

His grandfather, Daniel Jones, had been a member of a Wesleyan congregation; his grandmother, Mary, had joined the Calvinistic Methodists. His father, the Nonconformist minister, Michael Jones, had been a farm labourer and a stonemason. After he had obtained some schooling, with the help of a brother, Evan, Michael Jones was apprenticed to a bookbinder in Lampeter. When he was twenty, he was encouraged to start preaching, and worked to pay his way at Wrexham Academy, ultimately becoming minister at a chapel in Llanuwchllyn.

Nonconformity, which came into existence in the 17th century, was, in Wales, a way of life as much as a religion, for those who adhered to it; and its language was Welsh. Once persecuted for their dissention from the Established Church of England, so much so that a group of Quakers sailed on a ship called the *Mayflower* to a land that guaranteed religious tolerance, Nonconformist chapels were frequently targets for hostility. Worship in chapel, as opposed to worship the Anglican Church, was frequently punished by landlords, who increased rents. Its ministers were ordinary men, in ordinary trades, who turned to preaching and teaching. Their sermons were frequently debates on theological issues or, more and more, vociferous protest at the social conditions prevailing in Wales.

The Wales into which Michael D Jones was born was a land of religious dissent and political radicalism. In the years preceding his birth, Welsh Nonconformists of every denomination were seething with theological controversy and the injustice of having to pay tithes to the Established Church of England, used to swell the revenues of English bishops, or to glorify cathedrals such as those at Winchester, Gloucester, Windsor, Chichester or Worcester. Throughout his infancy, childhood and adolescence, Michael D Jones saw his father embroiled in a bitter fight for his ministry and arguments over Original Sin, which he denied, and the universality of Redemption, which he affirmed. Rather than denying his convictions, Michael Jones left his chapel, taking most of his congregation with him, and his home became the place of prayer meetings and theological discussion. Deprived of his ministry, Michael Jones taught in a small school, which, in time, his two sons and three daughters attended.

All the early education Michael D Jones and his brother and sisters received was from their father. By the age of twelve, Michael D Jones knew the fundamentals of Greek and Latin, and soon he was helping his father teach the other students.

Perhaps Michael D Jones had seen too much of the religious disputes in which his father had been so fiercely embroiled to want to follow in his footsteps; and, at first, philosophy intrigued him more than theology. Perhaps, too, being young and of a somewhat fiery disposition himself, he wanted to make his own way in the world, out of his father's shadow. For whatever reason, when he was fifteen, he decided to apprentice in a draper's shop in Wrexham, where he stayed for only a few months. Measuring, cutting cloth and selling spools of thread was not for him. He could not deny his destiny, and when he was sixteen, he decided to study to become a minister, too.

In the 19th century, poverty in the rural and industrial areas of Wales was extreme. Higher education, other than theological training, did not exist. Farmers were subject to increasingly higher rents from landlords, who were often absentees, and threatened with eviction, if they failed to vote for whatever parliamentary candidate the landlord supported. Almost all the constituencies were represented by the landowning gentry, who sat on local councils and dominated every aspect of local government. The demand for tolls on what had previously been public roads was a further cause for resentment that sometimes led to open rebellion. Common lands were being enclosed, restricting grazing and access to markets, forcing many to relocate to industrial towns like Liverpool, Manchester and London, or to emigrate.

As Michael D Jones grew to manhood, he saw his language being scorned by the English and by the anglicized Welsh, who considered the language to be a barrier to advancement and who were increasingly controlling every aspect of Welsh life. Westminster ruled that children in Wales should not be taught through the medium of Welsh, but through English, a language that was completely foreign to those who came from monoglot Welsh-speaking families; children who spoke it in the playground or classroom were punished and held to ridicule. Inevitably,

LETTSOME & SONS.   LLANGOLLEN

Michael Daniel Jones and Anne Lloyd Jones with Eluned Morgan,
daughter of Lewis Jones.

Welsh was declining and, with it, its literature and traditions. His blood boiled with rage that the land of Wales was owned by the gentry, who, by English law, also owned the minerals that lay beneath the soil. Slate and coal became more profitable than rents for farms. More and more, he saw previously rural areas like the Rhondda Valley and Merthyr Tydfil, Aberdare and Mountain Ash change forever, as seam after seam of the most sought after coal in the world was discovered. Rural life as he knew it vanished into the pits and caverns that scarred the hills into which men and boys, dispersed from the land, disappeared to work from dawn to twilight, from seven years of age – sometimes even five – until they died of diseases from the coal dust and poisonous gasses.

When Michael D Jones was seventeen, his father was reinstated in the chapel. When he was twenty, his parents moved to Bala, where his father was given charge of a new college for training students for the ministry, which had started the previous year, in Llanuwchllyn. It became known as the Independent College. By then, Michael D Jones was in training for the ministry, at the Presbyterian College in Carmarthen, the only form of higher education open to him in Wales. After four years at Carmarthen, he was accepted for further theological studies at Highbury College in London. With his studies in London completed, he had to decide what to do next. He received offers to serve in churches in London and Wales, but decided to travel to the United States, to see for himself how democracy worked.

He established himself in Ohio, where there were many Welsh communities. When he was twenty-five, he was ordained minister in the Welsh church at Cincinnati, Ohio, where he remained for three years. Emigration from Wales was constant, and he played a prominent part in forming an association for helping Welsh immigrants, especially newly-arrived, monolingual Welsh, for whom he acted as interpreter, and in finding employment and accommodation for them. The young minister soon observed that, although many among the first generation of Welsh emigrants kept their language and traditions, attended Welsh-language chapels and read Welsh-language newspapers, their children did not and were being assimilated into the culture of their adopted country. Emigration from Wales was a flood that could not be turned. What, he wondered, would be the result if that tide of emigration could be directed to somewhere that was remote from English influence, the English language and English rule?

He returned to Wales and, on the death of his father, became Principal of the Independent College at Bala. One of his students was Abraham Matthews, who was to become, with reservations, one of the main supporters of a Welsh colony in Patagonia. Another was Lewis Humphreys, who was also to become an important person in the colony.

In 1859, he married Anne Lloyd, the only child of John and Mary Lloyd of Bodfari, Flintshire, near Denbigh. Her father, a Lloyd of the Llwydiaid of Cwmbychan, in Merioneth, died when she was young, and her mother remarried. Her stepfather was a farmer, a cousin of John Lloyd, a trustee of his will and legal guardian of Anne and her mother. From her father Anne Lloyd inherited the property rights and the dwelling houses and adjoining lands of Rhosesmor, in the parish of Northop, Flintshire, and Cae Gwydd, in the township of Treuddyn, in the parish of Mold. On her mother's death, she stood to inherit another large farm, Tynyffordd, in Cymbychan.[14]

It was Anne Lloyd Jones's inheritance that enabled Michael D Jones to finance *Mimosa*'s voyage to Patagonia and establish the Welsh colony there.

A Colony

A colony where the Welsh would be free to make their own laws, speak their own language and follow their own traditions was not a new idea. A man named Morgan Rhys was the first to suggest the idea of a Welsh colony, by selecting Ohio as a place to which to emigrate. Before that, Quakers from Wales had joined their fellow Quakers in Pennsylvania, with the hope of being permitted to form a separate colony there – a request which, however, was not granted. There had been attempts to establish a Welsh colony in Tennessee; and places such as Wisconsin, Oregon, parts of South Africa, Vancouver Island, Australia, New Zealand, Uruguay and even Palestine were at various times considered and rejected. In 1848, Welsh Mormons emigrated in considerable numbers to Salt Lake City; and, in 1852, a small colony was established in Rio Grande do Sul, in southern Brazil.

By 1856, Patagonia was being considered by the Welsh in North America. In 1858, a carpenter called Hugh Hughes moved to Liverpool from Caernarfon and, in the following year, gave a talk in the basement of a chapel in Bedford Street, in which he spoke of Patagonia as the ideal place for a Welsh colony. Although the audience was sparse, the idea attracted two brothers called Williams, from Birkenhead, a cabinet maker called Maurice Humphreys, and a surveyor called William Davies, who, seven years later, would all sail, with their families, on *Mimosa*. A young printer, originally from Caernarfon, Lewis Jones, would become the first leader of the colony. They met at nights, after work, in a house in Williamson Square that was owned by two brothers by the name of Edwards, who, although they agreed to lend their ardent support to the venture, would not be among the passengers to sail to Patagonia.

The movement gathered momentum when Michael D Jones gave his support, because of his growing influence within Wales.

Patagonia, a vast, empty territory, five times the size of Britain, where no flag flew, would not be just a colony, but a place that would be subject to no laws but their own: a Wales without an England and its language, a Wales without taxes, tithes or landlords. Patagonia belonged to no one, since Argentine territory extended only as far south as the Rio Negro. It was seen to be the only hope of stemming the relentless tide of Anglicisation engulfing the rural and industrial towns and villages of Wales, or of assimilation into the vast melting pot of North America, a land that guaranteed freedom for everything, except the survival of their language.

The following year, in 1861, Edwin Cynrig Roberts, who had gone to Wisconsin from Cilcain, a small village near Denbigh, disembarked at Liverpool. A brilliant orator, he was an ardent supporter of the idea of founding a colony in Patagonia. That winter, a meeting took place in Hope Hall, and, on July 9, 1861, an Emigration Society was formed, consisting of prominent Welshmen living in Liverpool.

Application for land for a Welsh colony in Eastern Patagonia was made by the Welsh Emigration Committee to the Argentine consul in Liverpool, Mr S R Phibbs, an Englishman with business interests in Argentina, and won the enthusiastic support of the Minister of Interior of the Argentine Government of Bartolomé Mitre, Dr Guillermo Rawson, a former professor of medicine at the University of Buenos Aires and son of a New England physician who had settled in Argentina. His Argentinian mother was from a wealthy family in the province of San Juan. Lewis Jones and Thomas Love Duncombe Jones Parry of Madryn Castle, in the Llŷn Peninsula, were elected to negotiate terms with the Argentine government and to survey the land in Eastern Patagonia for possible settlement. Lewis Jones arrived in Buenos Aires at the end of November of 1862, Jones Parry a month later.

With letters of introduction from the Argentine government, they reached the then southernmost settlement of the country, Carmen de Patagones, on the Rio Negro. Unable to travel overland into Patagonia on horseback because of the drought and heat, they hired a 25-ton schooner, *Candalaria* from a man who had been a pilot in Darwin's expedition, and sailed four hundred miles south along the coast. A sudden storm forced them to take shelter in New Bay, a natural, semicircular harbour, which was an excellent anchorage. From what would later be called Porth Madryn, they sailed the forty miles further south, to where the river Chupat flowed into the sea. From there they travelled a further twenty-five miles upstream. The valley of the Chupat appeared to have everything required for a settlement. The land on either side of the winding river appeared to be fertile, and it was isolated. However, a dangerous sandbar across the mouth of the river made landing there impossible. A ship would have to anchor to the north, in New Bay, where the passengers could disembark and from where they would have to trek to the valley.

In Buenos Aires, an agreement was signed whereby the government guaranteed to make grants of land and livestock to the settlers. It did not, however, grant rights to self-government. Twenty-nine years before, in 1833, Britain had seized the Falkland Islands, expelling the Argentine governor, Louis Vernet; and Congress was suspicious that a colony from Britain, albeit a Welsh-speaking one, was an English conspiracy designed to take over and occupy Patagonia too. Rawson was, therefore, not in a position to grant all that the Welsh committee wanted. So eager was the committee in Liverpool to establish the colony in Patagonia that they accepted whatever was offered, which was one hundred acres of land per family and the promise of livestock and seed.

Later that year, 1862, a company was set up in Liverpool with the object of raising £50,000 by offering 5,000 shares at £10 each, in order to charter, buy or make ships to transport immigrants to the place; and Patagonia as a place in which to settle was promoted and extolled from pulpit, by pamphlet and by word of mouth, throughout the length and breadth of Wales.

Thomas Love Duncombe Jones Parry

Although he was not among *Mimosa*'s passengers, the name of Love Jones Parry is inseparable from the movement with which *Mimosa*'s name is forever linked and of the place destined to give her immortality.

When Michael D Jones failed to make progress in his endeavours to gain recognition for the Welsh Colonial Movement to Patagonia, he was advised by the consul, Phibbs, to set up a group of five respected and influential men to act as trustees. Their names, he was advised, should be well known, in order for them to appeal to a wide public, and they should have contacts able to open the necessary doors. In a few days, Michael D Jones had four names to add to his own: David Williams, High Sheriff of Merionethshire; G H Whalley, Member of Parliament for the county; Robert James, a prominent coal-mining owner from Wigan in Ohio, who was an uncle of Edwin Cynrig Roberts; and Thomas Love Duncombe Jones Parry, High Sheriff of Caernarvonshire and a rising political figure within the Welsh Liberal Party.

Unlike Michael D Jones, Sir Love Jones Parry, as he later became, was an aristocrat. From his father, also called Sir Love Jones Parry, he had inherited the fourteen-thousand-acre castled estate of Madryn, near Nefyn, on the windswept Llŷn Peninsula in North Wales. The dishes at Madryn Castle were of gold and silver. Paintings by Gainsborough, Reynolds, Holbein and Van Dyke hung on the walls. Every window bore the family coat-of-arms. He owned a residence near St James's Palace in London, and was a friend of the Prince of Wales, whom he entertained in lavish style at Madryn, along with the royal entourage. He was an inveterate gambler and once placed £8,000,000 on a horse in the Derby, and lost. Love Jones Parry travelled extensively in Europe, and was once imprisoned and sentenced to death in Spain for using his whip to attack a sentry at the border with Gibraltar. Only the intercession of Queen Victoria saved his life.

Despite the excesses of his lifestyle, he was known to be a good landlord, rarely raising the rents of his tenants, among whom he always spoke Welsh, the only squire in Caernarvonshire who did so. Also rare among landlords, he was a Liberal and not a Tory. He had a love of Welsh poetry, participated in local *eisteddfodau*, was a friend of the poet Talhaiarn, and adopted the bardic name, Elphin. When a renowned preacher and farmer, John Owen, was persecuted for his views and evicted from his farm near Bangor, Love Parry Jones gave him life tenancy of the best farm on the Madryn estate.

With aspirations to a Liberal seat at Westminster and his family's high standing, Love Jones Parry's endorsement of a settlement in Patagonia was important to the movement. Not only did his involvement give the movement a great deal of credibility, but he was admirably suited to liaise with the Argentine government. He contributed £750 so that he and Lewis Jones could travel to Argentina, to survey land for possible settlement and to discuss terms with the Argentine authorities.

Whether or not it was a condition to his involvement in the venture, the place where *Mimosa*'s passengers would disembark was given his name. It is questionable whether Love Jones Parry ever saw the place; he preferred the clubs and pleasures of Buenos Aires to the desolation of Patagonia, and not one of his tenants was ever encouraged to emigrate there.

Mimosa's People

Sixty-one-year-old John Jones, a collier from Mountain Ash, decided to take his wife, Elizabeth, their twenty-year-old son, Richard, their younger daughters, Ann and Margaret, and the sixteen-year-old boy, Thomas Harries Jones, who lived with them, to Patagonia. His oldest son, John, secretary of the Welsh Emigration Society in Mountain Ash, and his son's wife, Mary, expecting their first child, would accompany them. So would his oldest daughter, also called Mary, who was married to Daniel Evans, also a collier.

★

Daniel and Mary Evans had two young children, Elizabeth and John Daniel. They had charge of two young orphaned boys, William and Thomas Tegai Awstin, who, at seventeen and eleven, were already working in the mines with Daniel Evans, as their father had. The boys would also go to Patagonia with their adoptive family.

★

Rachel Jenkins was the second wife of Aaron Jenkins, who was also a collier in Mountain Ash. She was still nursing her youngest son, Richard, and was pregnant with her third child. Their elder son, James, was two years old and suffered from a condition known as *cancrum oris*, for which there was no known cure. The lower part of his face was sloughing away, and in time would expose his teeth and mandible bones. His death from infection or septicaemia was only a matter of time.

★

Thomas Williams was sixty, his wife, Mary, fifty-five. They had worked hard all their lives and had money in the bank. Although neither was in good health, they decided to emigrate to Patagonia where, it was said, they would never hear English spoken again.

★

John and Cecilia Davies, aged twenty-six and twenty-four, had a baby son. Not for him, they decided, would be a life in the coal mines. They would give him, and themselves, a better life in Patagonia.

★

Thomas Harris and his wife and four children, a young couple, James and Sarah Jones with their two young children, three unmarried women and six single men also decided to leave Mountain Ash and emigrate to Patagonia.

★

Abraham Matthews, a former theological student of Michael D Jones, living in Aberdare, in South Wales, was one of the three ministers who would accompany *Mimosa*'s people to Patagonia. In his early thirties, he had a wife, Gwenllian, and an eight-month-old baby daughter. His wife's younger brother, living in Bridgend, John Thomas, later to be known as John Murray Thomas, would accompany them.

★

Forty-year-old Thomas Davies, also from Aberdare, had been widowed, as had his second wife, Eleanor. Each had four children by their previous marriages, making a family of ten. All ten would sail to Patagonia.

★

Evan Davies from Aberaman, decided that he would take his young wife, Ann, and their fifteen-month-old daughter, Margaret Ann, to Patagonia.

★

Mary Ann John, alone and unmarried, decided that her savings would purchase a one-way ticket to a new life.

★

Joshua Jones from Cwmaman would also go out to Patagonia.

★

In Llanfairfechan, a fifty-one-year-old, widowed Baptist minister, Robert Meirion Williams, who had been a carpenter in the Crimean War, informed his adolescent son, Richard Howell Williams, that he had purchased two tickets for a ship bound for South America.

★

William Jones was a young tenant farmer of a small holding on the Rhiwlas estate, near Bala, on which he kept some cows, pigs and a few sheep. Before turning to farming, he had been apprenticed to a tailor. Before her marriage, his wife, Catherine, from the parish of Llandrillo, near Corwen in Merioneth, had worked as a milliner in Bala. They had two small daughters: Mary, who was not yet three, and Jane, who was born in March, 1864. Jane's birth had been difficult and beyond the skill of the midwife, necessitating the assistance of a doctor whose fees William Jones could ill afford.

After payment of his rent of £37, payment of tithes of £10 to the church he did not attend, and chapel funds to the one he did, there was little left of his annual income of £53 from the animals and wool he managed to sell. His family could only survive by the work he did, shearing sheep and working on a neighbouring farm at harvest time. The occasional tailoring job brought in an additional £2 a year, while Catherine churned the butter she sold at the weekly market in Bala. Their living was precarious and they found it hard to make ends meet.

When William Jones heard about a venture being proposed by the minister of Llanuwchllyn to emigrate to Patagonia, where families would be given free land, he decided that, wherever it was, Patagonia would be the answer to his prayers. The next time the minister spoke in his own chapel in Bala, William Jones would ask him for details of the proposed settlement in Patagonia.

★

Maurice Humphreys lived in Ganllwyd, near the granite-grey town of Dolgellau, and had been one of the early supporters of the idea of a Welsh settlement in Patagonia. His wife, Elizabeth, whose father was the Anglican bishop of Cardiff, was pregnant with their first child. His twin brother, Lewis, a minister who had been a student of Michael D Jones, and younger brother, John, would go with him and Elizabeth to Patagonia, leaving their elderly parents to pray that at least one of their sons might return to Wales before they died.

Maurice Humphreys was a cabinet maker, and one of Elizabeth's brothers was governor of one of the states in Australia. A branch of Elizabeth's family, whose name was Adams, was descended from two presidents of the United States of America: John Adams and his elder son, John Quincy Adams. She was related by marriage to Anne Lloyd, the wife of Michael D Jones. It is unlikely that her father approved of Maurice Humphreys' decision to settle in Patagonia, but Elizabeth supported her husband's desire for the Welsh traditions and language to be preserved, whatever the cost, and that their first child would be born in Patagonia.

★

Rhydderch Huws was journeyman joiner in Chorlton upon Medlock, in the borough of Manchester, where both work and misery in the cotton mills were plentiful. A widower of dark good looks with a young adolescent daughter, Jane, he had remarried five years before, when he was twenty-eight, possibly to provide a mother for Jane. His second wife, Sarah, was nine years his senior and had been a servant in Llansilin, Denbigh, where she had been born. They had a son, Meurig, four years old. Rhydderch Huws decided that they would leave the filthy slum tenements of Chorlton upon Medlock and go to a place where he would be master of his own destiny and subservient to none.

★

Thomas Pennant Evans, nicknamed Twmi Dimol, also living in Manchester, decided that he, too, would go to Patagonia.

★

Twenty-year-old Joseph Seth Jones was employed in Denbigh as a typesetter at *Baner ac Amserau Cymru*. Despite the cautionary advice of his six brothers, the distress of his stepmother and the violent opposition of his father, a lay preacher in the Presbyterian Church in Abergele, Joseph Seth Jones decided that he would avail himself of the free land offered in Patagonia. Prudently, he waited until after he had received his wages before he gave notice to his employer, Robert Gee. That very afternoon, he left Denbigh by train.

★

In Caernarfon, Stephen Jones, the eighteen-year-old brother of the future leader of the colony, informed his friend, Richard Hughes, that he would soon be departing for Patagonia, to join his brother Lewis. Richard Hughes decided that he would accompany him.

★

David Williams, whose mother had died some years before, was a shoemaker in Aberystwyth. He was twenty-one. With his friend, Lewis Davies, who was married with a small son a few weeks old, David Williams decided to leave the town with its face to the sea and its back to the hills for a land where, it was said, cattle grazed in green pastures beneath trees laden with fruit. Although he would be sad to leave his widowed father and sister, David Williams could barely contain his excitement. John Morgans, whose father owned a farm in Pwllglas, near Aberystwyth, would go with them.

★

John Williams had moved to Birkenhead, where there was more work for a carpenter than there was in Dolyddelen. He and his wife, Elizabeth, had a four-year-old son and a two-year-old daughter, also called John and Elizabeth. John Williams had skill as a bonesetter and knowledge of medicinal herbs. A quietly spoken man of thirty-six, and respected for his goodness, he gave freely of his services to those who requested them. His conviction that Patagonia would give his family a better life made him decide that they should move again.

★

Watkin William Pritchard Williams was thirty years of age and also living in Birkenhead, where his father, a retired ship's captain, had died three years before, in 1862. Together with his younger brother and sister, Watkin Wesley Williams and Elizabeth Louisa Williams, he decided that he would emigrate to Patagonia.

They had an uncle, John Jones, who had adopted the bardic name of Talhaiarn. John Jones was one of the architects employed in London in building the Crystal Palace, one of the wonders of the 19th century, and was cynically opposed to his nephew's determination to emigrate to Patagonia. He wrote to tell him so on Good Friday of 1865, from his house in London.

… Of all the wild, mad schemes that have turned up of late, the wildest and maddest is the Patagonian scheme. I may as well hold my tongue. Therefore I can only hope – hoping against hope – that you will all be successful, comfortable and happy. I also hope that the Indians who will eat you all bodily (will suffer) a confound indigestion.[15]

★

In Llandrillo, Catherine Davies was more concerned with the size of her youngest son's head than with her husband Robert's decision that they should emigrate to South America.

A victim of water on the brain, or hydrocephaly, little John Davies' body seemed too small to support the weight of his head. He had to be manually turned from side to side in his cot; he could not sit without his head being supported. Moreover, his eyes had begun to bulge, as if his brain was pushing them out, and his constant, high-pitched wails kept the two older boys awake at night. Sometimes he screamed violently for an hour or more, until he fell into an exhausted torpor, and more than once he had had fits.

Catherine Davies did not care about being free to speak Welsh in Patagonia. She just wanted John to get better.

★

Ann Lewis was a servant in a house in Abergynolwyn. She was thirty-five years old. William Hughes, also from Abergynolwyn, was a stonemason. He was two years her junior and widowed, and both were illiterate. Either separately or together, they decided to emigrate to Patagonia.

★

From Bangor Robert Thomas decided to take his wife and their two little daughters, Mary and Catherine Jane, aged five and two, to Patagonia. A natural musician, he would take his harmonium, too.

★

Amos Williams, a seaman also living in Bangor, decided that he had had enough of working under vile-tempered masters and mates on voyages that took him away from his young wife and daughter for months at a time. With his savings and the wages he received from his last voyage on a ship called *Realm*, there was enough to pay for his wife Eleanor's ticket to Patagonia, while he would try to work his passage in whatever capacity he could.

★

In Liverpool, interest in the venture was keen, although not without controversy. Hugh Hughes, known by his bardic name of Cadfan Gwynedd, was one of the first to extol the idea of Patagonia as a place in which a large colony might be established. He had written a lyrical and largely inaccurate description of the Chubut valley, based on Admiral Fitzroy's account of the area, omitting anything that might discourage settlers from going. He had a wife with a twenty-year-old daughter from a previous marriage, and two young sons aged six and four.

His wife's brother, David Richards, owned a house in Union Street, where many of the passengers were accommodated prior to sailing. The ship that was expected to be ready for the voyage to Patagonia on April 25 was called the *Halton Castle*.

★

Despite Hugh Hughes' passionate attempts to inspire others to come, only a few were willing to leave their jobs in Liverpool for the uncertainty of Patagonia: two Jones boys, George and David; a brick-maker, Edward Price and his wife and two children; a young man named William Williams' two brothers by the name of Ellis' whose brother was also going; and a couple of single women.

★

"*We were married on April 13th, 1865,*" Richard Ellis of Llanfechain wrote in his diary, after he had married Frances Cadwaladr in a chapel in nearby Llansantffraed ym Mechain.

They intended to start their married lives in Patagonia, and left for Liverpool to await the *Halton Castle,* due to sail six days later. Both were aged twenty-seven.

Richard Ellis's oldest brother, John, with whom the couple were undoubtedly staying as they awaited the day of sailing, had a shop in Liverpool. Their brother, Thomas, a pharmacist and deeply committed to the ideals of a Welsh colony in Patagonia, also lived in Liverpool. The two older Ellis brothers would accompany Richard and Frances to Patagonia. Their brother, David, had already emigrated to South America and had settled in Uruguay some ten years before. He gave good reports of the opportunities in South America.

★

From other parts of Wales, too, some were drawn to the idea of settling in Patagonia: William Roberts, a young adolescent from Seecombe; James Davies from Brynmawr, who was a gifted poet; two families and two single men from Ffestiniog; John Hughes and his wife and four young children from Rhosllanerchrugog, along with his brother Griffith, who had recently moved his wife and three children to the collieries of Rhos from Llanuwchllyn; and another couple by the same name, William and Jane Hughes with their daughter, from Anglesey. They and others set out for Liverpool, intending to board the *Halton Castle*.

The Halton Castle

By the middle of April 1865 more than two hundred men, women and children had left their homes in Wales and Lancashire, and were in Liverpool, awaiting the 478-ton iron barque, *Halton Castle*, owned by the Blythe Brothers, expected to sail on April 25, to transport them to Patagonia. The *Halton Castle*, named after a castle that overlooks the Mersey, was built in 1862 for the lucrative South American west coast run, which involved sailing around Cape Horn.

By the end of April, the *Halton Castle* had not returned to Liverpool from its voyage to Valparaiso. In order to sustain themselves and their families in Liverpool, some of the would-be passengers had taken casual employment. Others, with the help of dwindling financial resources from the Emigration Society, were being accommodated with Welsh families living in Liverpool. Some, having second thoughts about emigrating to a place as isolated as Patagonia, or being influenced by the vociferous detractors in the Welsh and Liverpool newspapers, had returned to their homes in Wales or Lancashire. Unless the contingent gathered in Liverpool sailed at once, the whole venture was in danger of collapsing. Lewis Jones and Edwin Cynrig Roberts were already in Patagonia, making preparations to receive their countrymen. To find a ship with a master willing to sail to Patagonia without further delay was imperative, and with the *Halton Castle* still on the high seas, it was decided that another ship must be chartered as soon as possible, but finding one was not easy.

A natural choice would have been one of the many emigrant ships of James Baines's Black Ball Line. The Black Ball ships took emigrants to Australia and were able to accommodate hundreds of passengers on any one voyage. Through his Liverpool contacts, Michael D Jones approached Captain Thomas Williams, an associate of James Baines and a strong supporter of Welsh Methodist causes in Liverpool. Captain Williams, categorically refused to release any of the Black Ball Line ships for what he considered so foolhardy and dangerous an enterprise. In a letter published in *Yr Herald Cymraeg* the following year, on March 17, 1866, Captain Williams made no bones about his opinions of the venture.

At somebody's instigation the Reverend M. D. Jones called on me to consult regarding a ship to transport the first contingent after they were disappointed by the unavailability of the ship they had hired. I told them without hesitation that not even for five thousand pounds would I work for them, when they were sending the innocent creatures out to such a remote place, without enough preparation being made for them. I also said that no woman or child should on any account go out there until things had been organized for them.

(Ar anogaeth rhywrai galwodd y Parch M. D. Jones arnaf, i ymgynghori ynghylch llong i gludo y fintai gyntaf allan, ar ôl iddynt gael eu siomi yn y llong oeddynt wedi ei llogi. Dywedais wrthynt y pryd hwnnw yn ddibetrus na chymeraswn bum mil o bunnau am fyned dan eu cyfrifoldeb, pan yn anfon y creaduriaid diniwed

allan i'r fath le anghysbell, heb haner digon o baratoa ar eu cyfer. Dywedais hefyd na ddylasai yr un wraig na plentyn ar un cyfrig fyned allan hyd nes y byddai pethai wedi eu trefnu yno ar eu cyfer)[16]

How and why *Mimosa* was chosen to sail to Patagonia is not known, except that other ships were either unwilling or unable to go, or were too expensive. The shipping community, like any other, is restrictive: everyone connected to it knows everyone else. Patagonia was a strange and dangerous destination, to which few owners would have risked sending their ships, especially ships carrying passengers and with no profitable cargo. Everyone knew of Patagonia: it was a place where the seas around its southern, rocky tip, shaped like a malevolent finger beckoning ships to their doom, were so treacherous that only the larger clippers could navigate them. The notion of sailing to its eastern coast with passengers, especially women and children, would have seemed like madness. Nevertheless, the need for a ship to sail there would likely have been the talk of ship owners and master mariners in Liverpool, when they met in the Exchange to gather the latest shipping news.

It is possible that one of the Black Ball Line's most renowned master mariners, Austrian-born Antony Enwright, was the link. In 1848, Antony Enwright had been master on Robert Vining's *Reindeer*. Possibly, he mentioned to his former employer the need of a ship to carry passengers to Patagonia. He also knew Thomas Kemp, *Mimosa*'s first master, since he had been on the China Tea run with another of Alexander Hall & Sons' ships, *Crysolite*, in the years when Kemp had sailed *Mimosa* to Shanghai. Possibly, he told Thomas Kemp of Captain Williams' refusal to provide a ship for an extraordinary voyage to Patagonia; and he, in turn, might have informed William Killey. Alternatively, when Captain Williams had categorically refused to release any of the Black Ball line ships, Enwright might have felt sympathy for the Welsh cause and suggested to Michael D Jones that he could contact Robert Vining, whose ships were on the Liverpool to Brazil run.

Vining & Killey appear to have had no qualms about chartering their now-old clipper, when they met with Michael D Jones and the Emigration Committee. The timing was perfect. *Mimosa* had arrived back from her last voyage from Brazil at the beginning of April and, as yet, no orders for freight had been received for another voyage. They could charter her to carry the passengers to Patagonia, and, on her return, she could carry goods from one of the Brazilian ports back to Liverpool. The Welsh minister would bear the expense of refitting. It seemed an ideal and profitable arrangement.

For Michael D Jones and the Welsh Emigration Committee, *Mimosa* was the last, desperate hope. Without *Mimosa*, the dream of a Welsh colony in Patagonia might collapse.

George Pepperell

When a ship was chartered, the master had to comply with the orders of the charterer concerning the destination, and, for the duration of the voyage, the charterer's instructions replaced those of the ship's owners. Ships were hired for a fixed period, to be used, with limitations, as the charterer wished, and it was the charterer's right to instruct the master. Normally, the whole voyage was planned in advance, arrangements were made for return cargo, and where it should be sought. However, it was often difficult for anyone to control the master's actions once the ship had left port. The master's word was still law, and if he misinterpreted or abused his authority, there was little that either the owners or the charterers could do about it.

The master of *Mimosa* for her now-legendary voyage to Patagonia was a twenty-five-year-old man from Dartmouth, in Devon. George Pepperell was her youngest master and held a Certificate of Competency. He came from a renowned Devon, seagoing family.[17] His father, and some of his uncles, brothers and cousins had been masters of ships, some of which had been lost at sea, and he knew the dangers inherent in the profession he had chosen.

George Pepperell was born in 1839 and obtained his master's certificate in Liverpool in 1862, when he was twenty-three, just three years prior to taking *Mimosa* to Patagonia. He captained his first ship, *Commodore*, for two years, making voyages to Brazil from 1862 to 1864. *Mimosa* was his second ship, and his first two voyages on her had been to Brazil.

He was a devout Christian and church-goer, who ordered that no work such as washing of clothes be done on board on the Sabbath. He was entirely different from the old-style clipper masters like Trevanion Hugo, who drove their crews as hard as their ships. His handwriting, in sloping, even elegant, copperplate, shows that, unlike *Mimosa*'s previous master, Archibald Johnson, who was barely literate, he was well educated.

He knew the route to the Brazilian ports as far as Rio de Janeiro, but knew nothing of the seas further south. Anxious to assert his authority, he brooked no opposition to his orders, however irrational those orders were, and sometimes ignored the advice of those more experienced than he was. On him depended the lives of her passengers and crew.

The Doctor

The Welsh Emigration Society placed an advertisement in one of the Liverpool newspapers, asking for a doctor to accompany the settlers to Patagonia. Thomas Greene, a twenty-one-year-old doctor from Ireland, having completed his medical studies in Edinburgh in April, responded to the advertisement and was accepted for the post. It is not known whether there were any other applicants.

Thomas William Nassau Greene was born on January 8, 1844, on a family farm in County Kildare, forty-five miles south-west of Dublin. He was the second of seven sons; his father was the seventh of son in a family of thirteen children. Thomas Greene was ten when his father died. His mother was born on the Isle of Man. Of Welsh ancestry, she belonged to a dissenting religion, called in Ireland 'Separatism', which had, in effect, separated from the (Anglican) Church of Ireland. Its adherents met in a rented hall in Dublin for weekly meetings and Bible readings. Like Welsh Nonconformity and Methodism, Separatism advocated simplicity in all things. The schools Thomas Greene and his brothers attended were owned by Separatist schoolmasters, known to his mother.

When he was sixteen, he enrolled at the Royal College of Surgeons in Dublin, physicians and surgeons then being educated separately, the surgeon holding a much lower position in the medical profession than the physician. The Royal College of Surgeons of Ireland was ranked as one of the most enlightened medical schools in Europe, requiring of its students a greater range of knowledge than most other colleges. He qualified in 1862, when he was eighteen, obtaining his Letters Testimonial. For the next two years he worked as an assistant in a dispensary practice. (The dispensaries were forerunners of state medicine; the patients were seldom charged, or were charged very little, for medical treatment.) When he was twenty, he went to Edinburgh, where, in April 1865, he obtained a post-graduate diploma in medicine from the Royal College of Physicians. By May, he was in Liverpool and looking for a position abroad, possibly as a ship's surgeon, like his older brother, John, who was a ship's surgeon with the National Steam Navigation Company on the Liverpool to New York run.

It is not known how or why he decided to sail to Patagonia as doctor to the colony. The idea must have intrigued him, as so few had ever been there before. In personality, he was a serious-minded young man, responsible with his older brother for the education of his younger brothers, who were still in their teens, and he satisfied Michael D Jones as to his character. Coming from a farming family, he fully intended to remain in Patagonia and avail himself of the free grant of land, as well as carrying out his duties as doctor to the colony.

A contract between Thomas Greene and Michael D Jones was written on May 9, 1865, on blue notepaper carrying the address of 5, Tower Buildings West, Water Street, Liverpool.[18] In it, Thomas Greene offered his services as: "Surgeon to the Welsh Colony in New Bay for the period of twelve months from the date of sailing hence." By the terms of the contract, Thomas Greene was to receive free cabin passage outwards, one hundred pounds sterling for the period of his employment, and board and lodging in the colony.[19] The contract is drawn up in the handwriting of Michael D Jones, and both signatures are witnessed by a man called Henry Watson.

Thomas Greene boarded *Mimosa* three days before sailing, at 2 p.m. on May 25. Loaded into the hold, with his books and clothes, were farming implements; they included a plough with which to work the land to be allocated to him.

Refitting for the Voyage to Patagonia

What Michael D Jones and the Emigration Society thought of the ship offered to them is not known. They would have been accompanied on a short tour of inspection, probably by William Killey, and certainly by George Pepperell and a government port official, in order to estimate how she might be refitted to carry passengers that included women and children as well as married and single men. The various Passenger Acts instigated in 1842 legislated that all paying passengers were entitled to a bunk to sleep on that was six feet long and eighteen inches wide; regular rations of cooked food and water. There had to be separate sleeping accommodation for single men and women and space to where the sick could be taken, whether or not there was a doctor on board.

One thing is certain and that is that *Mimosa's* female figurehead did not meet with her charterer's approval, and it was removed on May 22, and replaced by a simple, carved scroll.[20]

In the Clarence Graving Dock, *Mimosa* was refitted to carry the passengers with whose destiny she was for ever after to be linked.

Accommodation and supplies were provided for 133 adults; the married men with families and the single women in one part of the ship; single men in the fore part of the lower deck, with iron bars and separate hatches to the upper deck, to ensure that there would be no mingling or nocturnal visits. (This left an estimated 29 young children who were not included, perhaps because they were babies or young enough to share their parents' berths and food rations.) Washing facilities were installed in the main deck, where the families and single women were accommodated. Coal was required for cooking and heating. In the absence of port holes, ventilators and skylights were fitted. Tables, chairs and berths were made, the planks of wood to be disassembled and taken ashore upon arrival at New Bay. A lifeboat, evidently old, was purchased and re-caulked. Water and food rations were also purchased and would have to be carefully allocated throughout the voyage. Space was needed for four privies – two each for men and women. Whether or not they were taken on board, space for six dogs was allowed.[21]

A document dated May 24th and signed by Pepperell lists the following fittings as completed:

Fittings supplied to the ship "Mimosa" belonging to the passengers:

All the Berths, Tables and Seats and Hospitals on Lower Deck.

Bulkhead dividing single men on Lower Deck, Hatches for do. & Iron Bars.

Four Between Deck ladders.

Galley passengers' caboose. Five ring bolts for do.

Three double water closets on Main Deck.

Three galvanized iron ventilators.

Skylights on Main Deck at after part of Galley.

Covers of Fore and Main and after hatchways.

Life Boat. Masts, Oars, Sails etc. belonging to her. Two windsails.

All of the 300-gallon water casks.

Forty tons of coal all lying in the Middle of the Ship.

George Pepperell, Jun.

Master.[22]

Bill of Receipt

According to the receipts still in existence, the cost of chartering, provisioning and refitting *Mimosa* was £1,708 – 8s – 9d, payment of which was the responsibility of Michael D Jones. (Far more that amount would be spent in the coming years, to save the colony from extinction.) He had an annual salary of £150, augmented by £15 from three of the other chapels at which he preached. He also had his family to maintain: four-year-old Myfanwy, three-year-old Llwyd and two-year-old Mihangel; and his wife was pregnant with their fourth child. He had undertaken responsibility for paying the passages of 250 passengers, whether they sailed or not, and those who were gathered in Liverpool had to be maintained until *Mimosa* was ready to sail.

These were anxious days for Michael D Jones as he scraped together every penny. He received a donation of £300 from the Edwards brothers of Liverpool, in whose house in Williamson Square the early ideas for a settlement in Patagonia were discussed. The rents from his wife's properties were not due in time to meet the payments, and two properties, one of which was the land on which Bodiwan stood, were mortgaged for £1000. Although some of the bills would not have to be paid until early 1866, the money was barely enough to meet them. It was not enough to buy a medicine chest. Had it not been for the brother-in-law of Hugh Hughes, David Richards, residing in Union Street, where many of the passengers were housed, *Mimosa* might have sailed without one. David Richards borrowed £30 on interest to pay for one. It was ordered from a pharmacy specializing in medicine chests, located on Old Hall Street, on the corner of Union Street. The bill for the chest and supplies was made out to Michael D Jones on May 25.[23] The medicine chest was delivered to the ship on May 26, two days before sailing.

Costs of Charter and Refitting

Charter .... £833 – 6 – 8

Fitting of berths .... 70 – 0 – 0

Stores for 133 passengers @ 60s each .... 399 – 0 – 0

Miscellaneous building materials .... 7 – 13 – 1

Timber .... 3 – 0 – 9

Iron and chain work .... 209 – 3 – 7

Coal .... 21 – 9 – 0

Lamps, lanterns, oil, wicks .... 37 – 7 – 0

Ventilators .... 1 – 7 – 0

Compass .... 15 – 0

41 water casks and water for 133 passengers ...... 69 – 16 – 6

Floor scrubbers, mop .... 7 – 6

17 guns and bayonets .... 12 – 15 – 0

Ladles, quart and pint measures .... 1 – 1

4 life buoys .... 1 – 19 – 0

Copper range .... 10 – 0 – 0

Chain, anchor .... 1 – 17 – 6

Tools (second hand vice, sledge hammer) .... 7 – 15 – 0

Medicine chest and supplies .... 27 – 18 – 0

Fee for steam tug "Contest", May 25 .... 1 – 10

Fee for steam tug "Toward Castle",

    from 11 am, May 26 for 2 to 3 hours .... 4 – 10 – 0

Copper pumps .... 33 – 10 –0

100 bags Chicago wheat, cartage, sacks and twine .... 47 –13 – 4

The Crew

On May 23, 1865, the *Agreement and Account of Crew* was signed, and *Mimosa*'s name, registration number and tonnage were listed therein. Having been re-measured and reclassified as a barque, her registered tonnage was 409 tons, which considerably reduced her official carrying capacity. George Pepperell, residing at 45 Upper Warwick Street, Liverpool, was named as master.

George Pepperell took on a crew of fifteen (eight of whom were engaged as seamen), only one of whom he had ever sailed with before, as well as three teenaged apprentices. Because *Mimosa* was carrying passengers, a purser, passenger steward, passenger cook and a surgeon were required, in addition to the normal crew. These were Thomas William Nassau Greene, who, although only 21, gave his age as 22, from Kildare, Ireland (Surgeon); Thomas Evans, aged 29, from Montgomery (Passengers' Steward); Amos Williams, aged 25, from Caernarfon (Passengers' Cook); and Richard Berwyn, aged 27, who had emigrated to New York from Merioneth (Purser) signed on on May 25.

Thomas Evans did not go on board and, two days before sailing, on May 26, he was replaced by Robert Nagle, the son of a custom's superintendent from Barmouth, who, although he was not Welsh, would remain in Patagonia.

Richard Jones Berwyn, who had lived in London and had emigrated to New York, was signed on as purser and, on the order of the Michael D Jones, served as unofficial interpreter between Pepperell and Thomas Greene and the Welsh-speaking passengers.

The passengers' cook, Amos Williams from Caernarfon, whose wife and daughter were travelling as passengers, was working his passage and would also remain in Patagonia.

Passenger Lists

Few passenger lists of any voyage exist prior to 1870, since they were not required by law before that date. There appears to be no passenger list for *Mimosa*'s voyage to Patagonia that was documented in Liverpool before the date of sailing, except for names of individuals or families, identified by the places from where they came, that were scribbled in the back of Michael D Jones's diary, such as *pobl y Rhos,* or simply *Bala.* In this diary, Michael D Jones notes that space for 152 passengers, 135 in the main deck, 17 in the fore deck, was approved by a government surveyor; this excludes those working their passages as crew members, and babies under a year old.

In the history of the colony, *Hanes y Wladfa Gymreig yn Patagonia,* which he wrote and published some thirty years after the voyage, Abraham Matthews lists 152 passengers, among which he lists the two men who had preceded the passengers, in order to make preparations for their arrival.

In the list that he compiled in 1866 for the British authorities, when a British ship, *Vesta,* visited the colony, Richard Berwyn lists 162 passengers, which includes twelve names that do not appear in Abraham Matthews' list, and also those who worked their passages.

In his book, *Yr Hirdaith,* published by Gomer Press in 1999, Elvey MacDonald also lists 162, including the four who were working their passages and the eleven-year-old servant girl of Ellen Jones, the wife of Lewis Jones, who was in Carmen de Patagones with her mistress at the time of sailing. His is the most accurate list to date, in that it documents the ages of the passengers, so that one can differentiate adults from children and children from infants.

Including those working their passages, 41 came from Mountain Ash, in South Wales; 18 from Aberdar; 11 from Rhosllanerchrugog, on the northeast Wales coalfield; 11 from the slate quarrying area of Ffestiniog;

7 from Bangor; 5 from Aberystwyth; 4 from Ganllwyd, near Dolgellau; 5 from Llandrillo; 4 from Anglesey; 2 from Llanfairfechan, in North Wales; 3 from Llanfechan, in mid Wales; 3 from Abergynolwyn; 4 from Bala; 2 from Caernarfon; 2 single women from Bethesda; 14 from Liverpool; 10 from Birkenhead; 5 from Manchester; and 1 each from Brynmawr, Tregethin, Seacombe, Denbigh, Bridgend and New York, making a total of 162.

Passenger Ticket

Each passenger who had purchased a ticket kept it safe. It bore *Mimosa's* name, intended date of sailing: May 15, and destination. The fare was £12 for adults, £6 for children, although inability to pay was not a barrier to those willing to go, and there was no cost for babies.[24] Many of the passengers had spent their fare-money and savings during the month's delay in Liverpool, and Michael D Jones financed those who could not now afford the fare.

One original ticket still exists.[25] It is the one issued to Abraham Matthews, who was travelling with his wife and infant daughter and his wife's brother, John Thomas, who later added 'Murray' to his name. A servant also travelled with them, making a total of four paying passengers, the infant travelling free.

It reads as follows:

CAMBRIAN EMIGRATION OFFICE, 41 UNION STREET, LIVERPOOL. PASSENGERS' CONTRACT TICKET: Ship: *Mimosa*, of 450 tons register, to take in Passengers at Liverpool for New Bay on the fifteenth day of May 1865.

I engage that the Persons named in the margin hereof shall be provided with a Steerage Passage to, and shall be landed at the Port of New Bay in South America, in the ship *Mimosa* with not less that 10 cubic feet for luggage for each statute adult, and shall be victualled during the voyage and the time of detention at any place before its termination, according to the subjoined scale, for the sum of £48 including Government Dues before Embarkation, and Head Money, if any, at the Place of Landing, and every other charge, except freight for excess of luggage beyond the quantity above specified, and I hereby acknowledge to have received the sum of £48 in full payment.

The following quantities at least, of Water and Provisions (to be issued daily) will be supplied by the Master of the Ship as required by Law; viz. – to each Statute Adult, 3 quarts water daily, exclusive of what is necessary for cooking the articles required by the Passengers Act; to be issued in a cooked state, and a weekly allowance of provisions, according to the following scale: – 3½ lbs. Bread or Biscuit, not inferior in quality to Navy Biscuit, 11 lb. Wheaten Flour, 1½ lb. Rice, 1½ lb. Peas, 2 lbs. potatoes, 1¼ lb. Beef, 1 lb. Pork, 2 oz. Tea, 1 lb. Sugar, ½ oz. Mustard, ¼ oz. black or white ground Pepper, 2 oz. Salt, 1 gill Vinegar.

N.B. – Mess Utensils and Bedding to be provided by the Passengers.

Signed. James Lamb. On behalf of JAMES LAMB, of Liverpool.

'LIVERPOOL, fifteenth day of May 1865.

Everyone travelling was advised to take a blanket, towels, knife and fork, tea and a tablespoon, a plate or two, a tin to raise water, a cup and a saucer rather large, a boiling pot, a quart tin, and one that will hold three gallons. In addition, every man was told to take with him 15 cubic feet of implements; tea and coffee, and British money for trading should also be taken, and that 'clothing worn in Wales will do.'[26]

Departure

Mimosa, was hauled from the Clarence Graving Dock[27] via the Clarence Half-Tide Basin, so called because ships could enter it up to three hours before high tide, into the Victoria Dock. The Victoria Dock contained over five acres of water area, and it is unlikely that *Mimosa* was the only ship being loaded there.

On Wednesday, May 24, George Pepperell and the mate, John Downes, together with the carpenter and second mate, went on board, once the loading had been completed

On the morning of Thursday, May 25, *Mimosa* was towed into the river by the steam tug *Contest*, when the tide was high enough to float her over the lock sill. She lay at anchor in the river, while her passengers and crew boarded from the landing stage, and the remaining documentation was completed.[28] Most of the remaining crew boarded, together with Amos Williams and Richard Berwyn.

The following day, on Friday, Robert Nagle, the replacement passenger steward, went on board, and on Saturday, the day before sailing, a Portuguese seaman from the Cape Verde islands, Antonio Silva, went on board, again as a substitute for a missing seaman. (At fifty-nine, he must have been a last resort, perhaps even crimped.) On the same day, the medicine chest was delivered by boat.

How long the boarding of the passengers took is not known. Once on board, they would have settled themselves into their cramped quarters, Richard Berwyn allocating the places. They took only the bare essentials for the voyage into their quarters; the rest of their possessions were stored in the hold.

Finally, by Saturday evening, *Mimosa* was ready to depart and would sail on the tide the following day.

Never before had *Mimosa* carried with her so many hopes and dreams.

Never before were there so many to see her off as on this, her most momentous and memorable voyage. This was not a voyage like those of the immigrant ships bound for North America or Australia. This was unique. It is impossible to imagine the feelings of apprehension, optimism, sadness or elation of those who boarded *Mimosa*. Many were going to Patagonia for reasons of poverty, and had nothing to lose in the venture but their lives. John and Cecilia Davies from Mountain Ash boarded without their baby son, who had died in Liverpool while awaiting the *Halton Castle*. (For Cecilia Davies tragedy struck again, when her young husband drowned in the Chubut, three months after landing, leaving her alone and widowed in Patagonia.) For some of the single women, Patagonia, wherever it was, presented a less bleak future than years spent as servants for whom marriage was not allowed. The teenaged and younger children travelling with their parents or step-parents were given no say in the matter. Opposition to the voyage must have raised doubts in the minds of some of those on board. For most, there was no turning back, no return should things work out badly. With *Mimosa*'s, their fates were sealed.

Most had never travelled beyond their towns or villages before. The young and inexperienced doctor had no one with whom to confer on the medical cases with which he would be confronted. He, too, must have had some reservations about the months and years ahead. No one knew, even Pepperell, how long the voyage would take, or what lay in store for them upon their arrival. All could only trust and hope and pray.

For *Mimosa*, as well as her passengers, it was a venture into the unknown. She had never sailed so far south. She did not know the currents. She did not know the winds. She was old for such a voyage as this.

It is impossible to imagine the feelings of Michael D Jones as *Mimosa* prepared to depart: joy that the dream of a Welsh colony in Patagonia that

153

would be like no other had become reality; how much more would he have to pay for the realization of it? Maybe, there was disappointment that the wave of emigration he had hoped to direct to Patagonia was less than a ripple, and that so many of the group were women with young children, that so few of the men were farmers, anxiety that the only doctor who had applied for the post was so young and, therefore, inexperienced, and that, not being Welsh, he was not expected to remain with them for long, unless he learned Welsh and took a Welsh wife.

Michael D. Jones did not witness the departure of *Mimosa*, for, on the Saturday, he left Liverpool with his wife, in order to preach at Bala on the Sunday, and returned to Liverpool on the Monday.

Gadewais i a'm gwraig Liverpool a'n llong "Mimosa" ar yr avon Mersey. Yr oidont i adail dranoeth am Patagonia, he recorded in his diary.

(*I left Liverpool with my wife with the ship 'Mimosa' on the river Mersey. They were to leave for Patagonia the following morning.*)[29]

The members of the Emigration Society, who had worked so long for this moment, would have been at Pier Head, together with friends and relatives of those on board. Thomas Greene's older brother, Dr John Greene, in Liverpool en route to another voyage to New York, was there to see his brother off.[30]

Prolonged farewells are the worst things for both the departing and those left behind, and the agony for *Mimosa*'s passengers and of those on the land, separated by the barrier of murky water, must have been acute. Doubtless, there were brave, too-wide smiles masking apprehension, and unashamedly moist eyes, as well as expressions of joy and euphoria.

On Sunday morning, May 28, 1865, the winds and tides being favourable and the port procedures being complete, *Mimosa* was in readiness to depart. The Red Dragon of Wales was raised and an anthem was sung to the tune of *God Save the Queen*, the sentiments expressing, not loyalty to the ruling monarch whose kingdom they were leaving, but joy for the new land to which they were travelling, where they would be free of oppression and poverty. *Mimosa* was attached to the steam tug, and a pilot boarded, who would guide *Mimosa* through the treacherous sandbars and mudflats of the estuary. There was a clanking of chains as the anchor was raised, and *Mimosa* was taken along the low-lying Lancashire coast, past the Perch Rock Lighthouse, towards St George's Channel and the open sea.[31]

"*We left the River Mersey for Patagonia on the ship* Mimosa," Richard Ellis, from Llanfechan and accompanying his two older brothers and bride to Patagonia, wrote in pencil and in English in his new leather-bound diary with a brass clasp.

The seven-thousand-mile voyage to Patagonia had begun. Whatever the outcome, *Mimosa*'s name would be linked with it.

The Voyage

During the morning of that first Sunday of the voyage, Pepperell conducted a short Anglican service. A Sunday school for the children was arranged for the afternoon, and a Nonconformist service for the evening. The sea was rough. Most passengers were seasick, and there was worse to come.

Next day, around four o'clock in the morning, *Mimosa* encountered a violent storm and driving rain off the Anglesey coast, which confined the passengers below.

Joseph Seth Jones recorded it thus in his diary:[32]

Dydd Llun, 29ain.

Yr oedd yn hynod stormus tua 4 o'r gloch y boreu. Parhaodd yn stormus ac i wlawio o'r boreu tan rywbryd cyn boreu ddydd Mawrth. Yr oeddwn yn bur sal trwy'r dydd, ac ni chodais o fy ngwely; ac ni chododd fawr neb arall.

(A storm rose around 4 o'clock in the morning. It continued with torrential rain that lasted until a few hours before the early morning of Tuesday. I was very ill all day and could not get up from my bed. There were very few who could get up.)

Mimosa's timbers creaked ominously as she plunged and rose in the waves, which flung spray over the deck. Such was the force of the storm that a lifeboat came out from shore, and offered to rescue the passengers and crew, an offer that was rejected by Pepperell. By the following day, Tuesday, the storm had abated, the torrential rain ceased, and the weather improved. Now in full sail, *Mimosa* passed the Scilly Islands, Cornwall and the Irish coast, under clear skies.

Two letters exist, from Lewis Davies and David Williams from Aberystwyth. Addressed "Ship *Mimosa*", they were written in cheerful spirits on board *Mimosa*, and given to a pilot boat off the coast of the Bay of Biscay for mailing on the mainland.[33]

June 2: Dear Mother and Father,

We are all well. We are off the Bay of Biscay. We are going at the rate of 11 miles an hour. All well. I and David and John Morgans, Rachel and Tom are well. I hope that you are the same.

On board the "Mimosa", off the Bay of Biscay. Lewis Davies.

Ship "Mimosa", June 2. Per Pilot Boat off the Bay of Biscay.

Dear Father, Brother and Sister,

I write to tell you, in haste, that we are all well on board our ship, and in good spirits. I have nothing to tell you in particular, other than we have been most successful and prosperous on our voyage. Lewis Davies and his wife and child are well. Gives you his best respect. John Morgans, Pwllglas, is well. Goodbye at present. In haste, David Williams.

Joseph Seth Jones, too, sent a letter to his brothers. The same day as the letters were written, five days after leaving Liverpool, William Hughes, a stonemason, and Ann Lewis, a servant, both from Abergynolwyn, were married by Lewis Humphreys, one of the three ministers on board. They were in their early thirties, and Ann Lewis was in the early stages of pregnancy, her child having been conceived in March or early April. Why they waited to marry until *Mimosa* was under way is not known.

Five days later, on June 9, Catherine Jane Thomas, the two-year old daughter of Robert and Mary Thomas from Bangor, died. The cause of death recorded in *Mimosa*'s log was croup.

Croup, characterized by a sudden, hoarse croaking sound and a barking cough on inspiration, is not in itself a disease, but a symptom of an underlying respiratory condition, such as broncho-pneumonia. It is caused by spasm of the muscles, or a narrowing of the larynx, or by a membranous growth obstructing the larynx or bronchial tubes. The onset is often at night or in the early hours of the morning, and may recur over a period of several nights. Faced with his first case of impending mortality, Thomas Greene would have moved the child to the cabin allocated to the sick, and carried out the usual treatment current, applying warm fomentations to the little girl's throat, in a desperate attempt to ease the spasms. On Saturday, June 10, little Catherine Jane Thomas was buried at sea. The event was recorded by Joseph Seth Jones.

Dydd Sadwrn, 10fed.

Claddu'r plentyn am 10 o'r gloch y boreu, trwy'r ei daflu i'r môr mewn box a wnaed i'r pwrpas, a cherig yn un pen iddo, i'r dypen o'i suddo o'r golwg.

(The burial of the little girl was at 10 o'clock in the morning. Her body was cast into the sea in a box made for such a purpose, with stones placed at one end so that it would sink.)

Pepperell read the prayer book service for the Burial of the Dead at Sea, while the grief-stricken father, Robert Thomas, bowed his head, longing, perhaps, for the solace of music from his harmonium, which was packed in the hold. Mary Thomas held the hand of their surviving daughter, five-year-old Mary, the tears that streamed down her face blurring the sight of the weighted coffin being tipped from a plank and slowly sinking to the bottom of the sea. The crew, whatever their nationality, religion and character, would have stood as silent witnesses, some crossing themselves as they bowed their heads, for none can remain unaffected by the death and burial of a child at sea.

It was the first time that a child had died on board *Mimosa*; it would not be the last. That same day, at ten o'clock in the evening, James Jenkins, the two-year-old son of Aaron and Rachel Jenkins of Mountain Ash, died. Rachel Jenkins was heavily pregnant with her third child. The cause of death recorded in *Mimosa*'s log was *cancrum oris,* a gangrenous inflammation of the face that afflicts young children, often as a result of some previous disease, such as scarlet fever or measles. One, or both, cheeks redden and swell, the commissure of the lips crack, and on the inside of the cheek is a greyish area that sloughs away, sometimes exposing the gums and teeth, some of which loosen and fall out. The breath has a foul odour, which certainly permeated the cramped sleeping accommodation on board. Death is often from septicaemia.

The next day, on Sunday, June 11, Mary Morgan Jones, also from Mountain Ash, was delivered of a son, Morgan, in one of the cabins allocated as a hospital. There is nothing as intimate as the birth of a child, save the conception of it. Every whimper, every gasp, every scream as the contractions increased, would have been heard. So, too, would the first, miraculous cry of the newborn. There is little doubt that, as the young mother cradled him in her arms, Morgan Jones's birth brought hope to the passengers and helped, in part, to alleviate the sadness that prevailed from the deaths of Catherine Jane Thomas and James Jenkins.

★

Sixteen days after leaving Liverpool, on June 13, *Mimosa* passed the island of Madeira. The passengers had never seen the tropics, or experienced such sultry, soporific heat. None had witnessed such spectacular sunsets, or seen the sparkle of phosphorescence in the foam of *Mimosa*'s wake after dusk, or such clarity of air. Although they were four or five miles from shore, they could see whitewashed houses thatched with palm fronds and hovels made of gorse-like vegetation built against the slope of a hill. They gazed at palm trees, blistering white sands and terraced plantations with wonder and amazement, as they strolled about on deck, their sleeves rolled up to their elbows in the heat, their faces reddening from the sun. Two days later, they saw in the distance the Canary Islands and the mountain of Tenerife.

The following day, on the hot morning of June 16, tempers rising with the temperatures, Pepperell discovered that the heads of some of the passengers were dirty. He decided that, in the interests of hygiene, possibly to prevent typhus carried by lice, the women's hair should be cut to the scalp and their heads washed with soap and water. A young adolescent girl on the quarter deck, Jane Huws, was unceremoniously seized by a member of the crew, shears in hand, intent on carrying out Pepperell's orders. At her scream of terror, other passengers rushed towards the quarterdeck to see what was happening. Her father, Rhydderch Huws, and Hugh Hughes confronted Pepperell, outraged, and demanded of him what he thought he was doing. Pepperell responded by drawing his revolver and threatening Hugh Hughes by pointing it at his chest. When Hugh Hughes refused to be intimidated, Pepperell raised his revolver and fired – into the sea. On Rhydderch Huws' passionate protests at the treatment of Jane, Pepperell ordered the mate, John Downes, to manacle him. Downes approached Rhydderch Huws with the iron handcuffs, jangling them and taunting him. Evidently reconsidering such a high-handed action, which would cause anarchy on board, Pepperell agreed to a compromise of sorts, whereby Thomas Greene and he would inspect the heads for lice; but from then on, he denied the passengers access to the quarterdeck, further restricting access to fresh air and space for exercise.

Thomas Greene's position on board was a difficult one. With so many people crowded into so confined a space, the risk of an epidemic was high. One case of typhoid fever or cholera, or any of the infections that were frequently contracted in Liverpool, would spread to the other passengers and to the crew, affecting especially the very young and the elderly. He was responsible to Michael D Jones for the passengers' health, as far as was possible, and, as a member of *Mimosa*'s crew, subservient to Pepperell. A ship surgeon's relationship with the master, who frequently interfered with and countermanded the surgeon's instructions, was not legally defined, and the limit of Thomas Greene's authority on board was hazy, at best. He was equipped with a medicine chest, which was the property of the colony, but the efficacy of its contents did not guarantee survival of the sick. (Among its contents was a bottle of thirty "spotted" leeches.) He spoke no Welsh, and had to rely upon Richard Berwyn, when examining the sick or delivering a baby. The births and deaths that occurred on board are recorded in the Official Log. Not recorded are the cases of seasickness and the other non-terminal cases that undoubtedly occurred.

On June 21, the passengers saw numerous sharks and caught a flying fish. Despite the presence of sharks, some of the young men plunged into the sea and allowed themselves to be towed on a rope tied around the bowsprit. As *Mimosa*'s prow rose and fell in the buoyancy of the waves, the young boys hanging onto the rope were alternately lifted above the waves and submerged below them.

The wind picked up, a little too strongly, and, on the afternoon of the following Sunday, *Mimosa* encountered a tropical storm. That same Sabbath, June 25, in the middle of the storm, the second baby was born on board. This was to Rachel and Aaron Jenkins who, just a fortnight before, had lost their son James. The baby was a girl, and they called her Rachel, after her mother. She was not destined for a long life.

Mimosa crossed the equator and passed imperceptibly into the Southern Hemisphere. To mark the occasion, there was a celebration of Crossing the Line, and much hilarity as the young male passengers were chased by the crew and had water thrown on them. Some of the passengers were invited to partake of drinks in Pepperell's cabin, and Joseph Seth Jones recorded incidents of drunkenness in his diary, although he himself was not present, being prostrated by seasickness.

Not all was merriment on that day, however, for John Davies, the eleven-month-old son of Robert and Catherine Davies from Llandrillo, died of complications as a result of hydrocephaly, described in the ship's log as: Water on the Brain.

Hydrocephalus is an accumulation of serum in the cranial cavity, a fatal condition in the 19th century. The head is enlarged, sometimes grossly, and there is separation of the bones of the skull. The forehead is exceedingly high, the veins of the scalp are enlarged and prominent, and the patient's eyes protrude. As the head enlarges, the body wastes away, emphasizing the size of the enlarged head, and the child cannot hold his head upright.

At the beginning of July, *Mimosa* entered the Doldrums, the region of calms between the Southeast and Northeast Trade Winds. The air became still, the sea like a millpond, and *Mimosa*'s sails hung limply

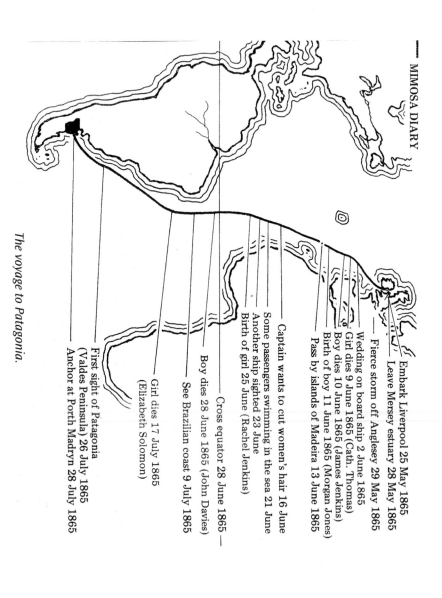

The voyage to Patagonia.

Embark Liverpool 25 May 1865
Leave Mersey estuary 28 May 1865
Fierce storm off Anglesey 29 May 1865

Wedding on board ship 2 June 1865
Girl dies 9 June 1865 (Cath. Thomas)
Boy dies 10 June 1865 (James Jenkins)
Birth of boy 11 June 1865 (Morgan Jones)
Pass by islands of Madeira 13 June 1865

Captain wants to cut women's hair 16 June
Some passengers swimming in the sea 21 June
Another ship sighted 23 June
Birth of girl 25 June (Rachel Jenkins)

Cross equator 28 June 1865 —
Boy dies 28 June 1865 (John Davies)
See Brazilian coast 9 July 1865

Girl dies 17 July 1865
(Elizabeth Solomon)

First sight of Patagonia
(Valdes Peninsula) 26 July 1865
Anchor at Porth Madryn 28 July 1865

around her masts. Water was even more severely rationed, for, unless rain from a sudden squall could be caught in an outspread sail, there would be none once the supply on board was exhausted. The heat became intense, especially below decks. The humidity was intolerable. Lethargically, the crew went about their tasks. Those accustomed to going barefoot or in canvas slippers, tied rags around their feet, for the heat on *Mimosa*'s decks was enough to melt the tar between her planks. The decks, when not bubbling with melted tar, continued to be holystoned with pumice, masts were greased for the easier raising or lowering of sails, and the ship tacked and re-tacked in the hopes of finding a breeze. The alternative was to haul her by ropes attached to a rowboat.

The passengers stood on the small deck space permitted to them, looking in vain for a sign of a wind that would speed them southwards. The glare off the sea burned their faces and was excruciating to their eyes.

Out of the Doldrums at last, the coast of Brazil was sighted. Some of the young male passengers lent the crew a hand by going aloft and reefing sails. For the next ten days little of note occurred on board. People gathered themselves into groups, and friendships and alliances were formed, which would remain after their arrival in Patagonia. Some were monolingual Welsh-speakers. Others spoke both Welsh and English. Wales seemed far away, Patagonia even further. *Mimosa* was the only reality, and it was the daily routines on board that became of prime importance.

As part of his duties, Thomas Greene ensured that everyone who could do so got up from their berths every morning and partook of the daily issue of lime and lemon juice, required by law on every ship as an anti-scorbutic. Those who were seasick were given something to settle their stomachs. Constipation from the salt meat diet and lack of fruit and vegetables became chronic, and faces broke out in boils. Scurvy could not be entirely kept at bay by the daily intake of lemon or lime juice. The women in the early stages of their pregnancies would have experienced morning sickness, the constant motion of the ship adding to their nausea and discomfort. Joseph Seth Jones complained in his diary of constant seasickness, and he was likely not to have been the only one. He also suffered from renal calculi.

Few had ever travelled beyond their own towns or villages, except to Liverpool to board the ship. Now, all were crammed in sleeping accommodation, where a makeshift curtain hung between the bunks provided the only semblance of privacy. Young girls, who knew no men except their fathers, grandfathers or brothers, now had to endure the lascivious glances and lewd innuendos of the crew and the agony of washing in public soiled or spotted undergarments. Perhaps they were conscious, too, that the future of the colony was dependent upon them marrying and bearing children, and that there were fewer of them than young men who would be requiring wives.

Mimosa sailed further south. David Williams, a twenty-year-old shoemaker from Aberystwyth, poured over the manual of the colony that had been written by Hugh Hughes, in a fervour of anticipation, perhaps, in the company of his friends, Lewis Davies and John Morgans, also from Aberystwyth. He made up an irreverent version of the Ten Commandments, adding an eleventh, which made them laugh.

The conditions were cramped in the extreme, especially after Pepperell restricted their access to the quarterdeck. The stench below decks from stagnant bilge water and too many people crowded in a too small and inadequately ventilated space must have been overpowering, especially when the temperature rose and the wind dropped.

Bed and personal linen, babies' napkins and clothes would have been washed in tubs of sea water, on the two days set apart in each week for washing clothes, and tied on the rails and rigging, or any available space below, to dry, giving *Mimosa* the appearance of a floating tenement. Stiff with salt when dry, the cloths and clothes caused rashes in armpits, necks and groins. The four privies would have been inadequate for the number of people that required them. Inevitably, tensions ran high and quarrels broke out, especially when rations of food were stolen or unfairly distributed.

At some point, Robert Nagle decided that he would remain with the passengers, when *Mimosa* anchored in New Bay. Richard Berwyn, purser, meticulously recorded the births and deaths in the ship's log. Joseph Seth Jones continued to record in his diary his queasy stomach, his constipation and diarrhoea, and his rage that some of his carefully-saved food had been stolen from his box.

By the middle of July, they saw the huge mouth of the Rio de la Plata, the widest river estuary in the world. On the fourteenth of the month, Mary Jones, the two-year-old daughter of William and Catherine Jones from Bala, came down with a heavy cold. Three days later, at 8 o'clock in the evening of the seventeenth, thirteen-month-old Elizabeth Solomon died of acute bronchitis, and was buried at sea on the following morning. She was her parents' only child.

Little Mary Jones's condition worsened and she developed a fever, which, too, turned into bronchitis and possibly pneumonia. At this point, or before, she would have been moved into the hospital cabin. With only a limited supply of medicines, there was little that a doctor could do, except apply a mustard poultice for ten minutes every three or four hours as a counterirritant, in the hopes that her little body would react and expel the secretions in her lungs that threatened her life. Her despairing mother would have been asked to sponge her face and body with tepid water, in an attempt to lower her raging fever, while the doctor watched for signs of the cyanosis or convulsions that were indicative of a fatal outcome. ·

Later that day, Pepperell ordered the mainsails to be raised to increase *Mimosa*'s speed. Evidently, there was a too-still calm on the sea – the veritable calm before the storm. Downes, the more experienced seaman, bluntly advised lowering them. Perhaps he saw the flashes of lightning and blackening clouds that forewarned of the pampero, the seasonal wind that blows across the pampas, to expend itself as much as four hundred miles out to sea. Finally, all the sails except two, to help keep her steady in the sudden scream of wind, were lowered and tightly secured, when the storm erupted. The passengers were ordered below, trapping them in whatever would be *Mimosa's* fate. The water that deluged the decks came through the cracks of the closed hatches, and flooded the passengers' quarters. The waves became mountains up which *Mimosa* climbed to the crest only to plunge into troughs so deep that her two sails went limp, while another mountain of water of towered above her. *Mimosa* creaked and groaned under the impact of the pounding to her hull, as she struggled to keep from being submerged or rolled over onto her side. Rachel Jenkins held her baby close to her, her face wet with the perspiration of terror. Others, paralyzed with fear, could only gaze at the lantern swinging above them in ever widening arcs, and pray. Under her sodden blankets little Mary Jones' condition grew worse.

The storm continued for three days, during which *Mimosa*, despite Downes' precautions, was swept three hundred miles off course, eastwards. On the third day, the danger was over, the sails were raised again and *Mimosa* limped back onto her course southwards. She was too old to take such a battering, and would not easily withstand another.

During the last week of the voyage, there was a chill in the air. The days were getting longer, and it was light by six o'clock in the morning. Perceptibly, the lapis-lazuli blue of the sea became a pale aquamarine, indicating that they were in shallower waters and approaching land. Flights of seabirds became more numerous, their cries more raucous. Terns and *pen wyns* bobbed on the surface like flecks of flotsam, as uncountable as the stars in the night sky. Unidentifiable scents of land and vegetation wafted on the air. Sometimes they caught the sound, or imagined it, of a dull rumble of waves breaking on an, as yet, unseen shore. They were nearing the end of the voyage.

The Landing

Half-way between Buenos Aires and the Strait of Magellan is a small, goblet-shaped hunk of land that juts out into the South Atlantic; so narrow is the thread of land that attaches it to the mainland that the Peninsula Valdés barely misses being an island. Salt flats shimmer white in the sun and lie one hundred and thirty-eight feet below the level of the sea, the lowest geological point of South America. Tidal flats are pink with flamingos or white with egrets. Walruses and giant elephant seals lie like petrified tree trunks on the sandstone shelves of rock. Sleek seals by the thousands recline on headlands of coves where tides rise to over eighty feet. Small flightless birds, guanacos, rheas and *maras* inhabit the arid wasteland of scrub and rock. Vast flocks of cormorants and gulls nest on its low, sheer cliffs. A narrow inlet, some twenty miles long, runs along its eastern side, separated from the open sea by barren mounds of surf-polished stones. The peninsula forms the northern boundary of the natural harbour called New Bay.

At seven o'clock on the morning of Wednesday, July 26, nineteen-year-old William Jenkins climbed the mast and saw land. Excitement ran high. At around midday, *Mimosa* sailed around the northern promontory of the Valdés Peninsula.

By three o'clock in the afternoon, they were just a mile from the peninsula. *Mimosa* was sailing well, and between five and six o'clock, all the sails were lowered, except for three or four. Their destination was now very close. Low, white hills, dark-capped with struggling vegetation, that were not like the green hills of Wales, extending from a seemingly endless plain, could be seen on both sides. At about ten o'clock that evening, they saw the entrance to New Bay. *Mimosa* sailed on. Apart from a skeleton crew, most turned in to sleep. While they slept, the second mate, Matthew Burgess, who had the wheel, steered dangerously close to one of the rocks, and there was fear that *Mimosa* would become grounded or suffer damage to her hull.

As *Mimosa* sailed into New Bay by moonlight, no pilot ship greeted her. No semaphore operators atop a lookout tower signalled her arrival, as at Anjer. Her sails gleamed pale in the moonlight as her green-coppered hull sliced the waves; the only visible motion was the white curl at her bow and an occasional toss of spray. She seemed to skim the surface of the water like a gigantic bird and, like a bird, abruptly began to fold her wings, as the studding sails came in from her sides, making her look leaner and trimmer, and her main sails were lowered.

Mimosa's cannon was fired to announce their arrival, and a responding salvo of gunfire from the shore, which put the myriads of seagulls to flight and made penguins and seals take refuge in the waves, indicated that their long-awaited arrival was seen. On the shore, Edwin Roberts who, with Lewis Jones, had been sent ahead to build huts and make preparations for the colonists, lit a fire on the cliff top.

Many could not sleep that night. Those who did found that, when they awoke, they were anchored in a natural, land-locked bay formed by a semi-circle of rocks eight feet wide and some twenty in length. Several got up at four o'clock and donned their Sunday clothes, waking those below as they paced the deck. The morning was clear and sunny, with blue skies, but with a nip in the air.

In the early hours of the morning of July 27, little Mary Jones died. She would be the first among them to be buried in Patagonia. She was a week from her third birthday.

As the sun rose higher, the passengers crowded to the rails, squinting towards land. There was no sign of Lewis Jones or Edwin Roberts, and so they feared that they had not come to the correct place. As *Mimosa* drifted towards land, someone sighted a dark smudge, like a cave. As it approached, they saw that it was a schooner. Just after midday, Pepperell, with four of the crew to row one of *Mimosa's* boats, elected Thomas Greene and twenty-seven-year-old Watkin Wesley Williams from Birkenhead to accompany him to the schooner.

Towards four or five o'clock in the afternoon, they returned with Lewis Jones, the leader of the colony, who had been preparing to sail to Carmen de Patagones to collect more supplies. Until only a few days before this, he had still been expecting to greet the *Halton Castle*. Eager hands helped him on board and joyful voices cheered him. He told them of the islands of guano that lay to the south of the mouth of the river and of the quarries of black marble in the north. There would be work for the men, he assured them. There were houses to be completed; fences to enclose the livestock to be made. There was land to be cleared and seed to be planted, although they were now too late to sow for this year's harvest. If any had qualms as they looked towards the desolate shore, they did not show them.

Mimosa sailed towards her anchorage, with Lewis Jones still on board. Later that day, Edwin Cynrig Roberts came on board, and some of the passengers prepared to disembark. It was decided that the men should leave first, followed over the next days by the women and children. Hugh Hughes was in the first boat, with Lewis Davies and David Williams from Aberystwyth, and Watkyn William Pritchard Williams and his brother

The landing.

Watkyn Wesley Williams from Birkenhead. Ignoring the ice-cold of the sea, Hugh Hughes plunged into the water and waded to the shore, so that he could be the first to reach land. Falling on his knees and weeping with emotion, he kissed the soil of Patagonia.

The landing of the first contingent was at a place they later called Fali Fawr, later referred to as Laguna de Derbes, and was where the town of Puerto Madryn stands today.

Upon landing, the young men started to explore inland, chatting amongst themselves. Eventually, they turned back and discovered that David Williams was not with them.

The following day, July 28, the main group of passengers disembarked and were brought to shore, leaving some still on board. A cold wind pierced their woollen coats and jackets, which were not made for the Patagonian winter, and an icy sleet began to fall. William Jones, his face grey with grief, carried the small coffin bearing the body of little Mary.

The women, especially the old and those who were pregnant, were helped ashore from the rowing boats and looked about them in bewilderment.

Sixteen unroofed huts, made of wood transported from Carmen de Patagones, were built into the shelter of the dunes. They were merely planks driven upright into the ground; each hut would accommodate eight at most, and would shelter them only from the worst effects of the wind and cold. Any cooking and ablutions would have to be done outside. The only source of water was three miles away, and would have to be carried across a muddy track, for the water from the well that had been dug at the site of the huts was found to be too brackish to be drinkable. A long wooden shed, built with the wood intended to roof the huts, after the storehouse of blocks cut from the soft tosca cliff had collapsed in the strong winds, held the stores of salted meat, sacks of flour, potatoes, and seed for planting that had to sustain the colony for the next weeks or months.

They were seven thousand miles from Wales and four hundred by sea from the closest settlement at Carmen de Patagones. Whatever the discomforts of the voyage, the sight of *Mimosa* anchored in the bay must have stirred feelings of some sort of security. The routine on board had, at least, been predictable. Here the only predictability was uncertainty and discomfort.

Children began to whimper and babies to cry. The women, their faces pinched with weariness and disappointment, tried to arrange some sort of shelter for themselves and their children. Their furniture, which some of the men were bringing in by boats from *Mimosa*'s hold, was strewn haphazardly on the beach. Was it for this that they had left Wales? How would they live in such desolation?

Edwin Cynrig Roberts, in his unpublished manuscript, *Mordaith i Batagonia* (*Voyage to Patagonia*), wrote of the morning of the landing thus:

The day of the test has arrived. Strong winds of disappointment begin to blow, tender-hearted mothers with their tears flowing having to make a bed for their children on the naked beach. The men are busily carrying the furniture to the land with the sea to their waists as they meet the boats and heap them here and there, and the mothers try and arrange some sort of shelter among the furniture.[34]

It was decided that, while those among them who had carpentry skills would roof the huts, the women with babies and young children would return to the ship. The others would be accommodated in the shed, men in one part, women in another.

Some of the younger women and girls who had not returned to the ship went in search of water. It began to grow dark. Night fell, and still they had not returned. In desperation, their names were shouted and fires were lit to signal the place where the men were gathered. Those on the beach undoubtedly cursed the day they had decided to come to Patagonia, as they waited, watched and prayed throughout the night. Already, David Williams was lost, for he had not returned.[35] Would their wives and daughters be lost, too, wandering in the desolation of the strange and empty land, with no familiar landmarks to guide them? By morning, the women had returned, tired, hungry and still thirsty.

Thus, ended the first day in Patagonia.

On Sunday, July 30, little Mary Jones was buried; Joseph Seth Jones dug the grave. The following day, Richard Berwyn, Amos Williams, Robert Nagle and Thomas Greene were formally discharged from the list of *Mimosa*'s crew and given their pay of a shilling a month, all the passengers having landed.

New Bay

The place where the passengers disembarked was suitable for a temporary abode, at best. Steep cliffs, into which the sea had eroded vast caverns that became partially submerged at high tide, rose from a stony beach to an elevated, barren tableland. The only vegetation was tough grass and thorn bushes that stretched from the shore westwards to the horizon and were impossible to walk through without tearing one's clothes and skin. Abraham Matthews described it thus:

The land around Porth Madryn is sandy and stony. There is neither a valley, nor a river, nor a stream, nor any source of water anywhere. The land is poor and rough and covered with small bushes.[36]

That part of Patagonia was inhabited only by nomadic tribes of Tehuelche Indians, who, following the migratory paths of the guanaco and ostrich to their seasonal feeding and breeding grounds, hunted in the eastern part of Patagonia from April to July, and spent the rest of the year in the Andean foothills. When *Mimosa* arrived in New Bay, the Tehuelche had departed on their journey westward.

Hunger became a permanent accompaniment to the cold and discomfort. Water from the well that had been dug close to the huts proved to be salty and unfit to drink. Ponds formed by heavy rain were some three miles distant along the beach from the huts; but the horses they had been given could not pull the barrels in the viscid mud and the oxen yoked to the cart could not drag it along. All water had to be carried in buckets. Some of the cattle and sheep that had been transported by Lewis Jones from Carmen de Patagones wandered away and could not be found; the boys elected to guard them had little experience in herding, especially in a land that was open and without boundaries for thousands of miles. Neither could they milk the semi-wild cows, to obtain for milk for the children. Sand blew into the food and gritted their faces; and the ceaseless Patagonian wind chilled them to the marrow.

Food was severely rationed. Much of it was wheat, which had to be ground to make flour. There was some rice and mutton, which consisted more of bones and gristle than edible meat; and the danger of scurvy was to intensify in the months that lay ahead. On board ship, there had been the daily ration of lime or lemon juice. On land, there was no supply of fruit or vegetables to prevent it.

Based on a letter written at the beginning December by Thomas Greene to "H.G.", likely, his younger brother, Henry, the following account appeared in the *Liverpool Mercury* on January 30, 1866:

On their arrival in New Bay the only place prepared as shelter for the immigrants was a long wooden shed not large enough to accommodate all, and men and women had to sleep, partitioned off, how they could, the rest shifting as best they might. Their food had to be cooked out of doors, which was constantly covered by clouds of sand and penetrating even their clothes. The water was scarce and bad, and had to be carried over two miles from a stagnant pool formed by recent rains, and was of a whitish colour from the marly nature of the soil and, moreover, was full of animalculae … The country he describes as being nothing but level plains as far as the eye can reach, covered with low stunted bushes much resembling the furze of our own country. The game, he says, is not much of any kind: some guanacos, foxes, etc. The birds are a species of emu, wild duck, etc., all hard to get on account of the level nature of the country … They were obliged to kill a horse for food; and he tells me that he was very glad to eat seagulls and owls, and says he killed a fox, but had not the good fortune to partake of its flesh.[37]

Laundry and personal hygiene had been difficult on board ship. It was even harder on land. Because of the difficulty in carrying water such a distance, soiled clothes and babies' napkins had to be carried across the mud and quagmires to the water, and washed there in tubs, or washed in the sea. Drying them would have been an even harder task.

Some of the women were pregnant: twenty-one-year-old Elizabeth Humphreys, in her ninth month, was expecting her first child; Ann Lewis, who had been married on board, was in her fourth month; Frances Ellis had conceived a child on the voyage and was in her second month. Even normal exertion tired them, especially those who had young children to care for. An elderly couple from Mountain Ash, who came alone, were too old and too frail for the difficulties that faced the colony, and it was too late to say that they should not have come. No one had clothes that were warm enough for the Patagonian winter. What they had, they wore; they took off nothing at night as they huddled together for warmth beneath the threadbare blankets they had brought from Wales. Children began to cough; noses began to run. They whimpered from the cold and hunger. There was no milk for the babies and infants, and the brackish water gave them diarrhoea. They needed warmth, to prevent coughs and colds turning into bronchitis and pneumonia. Should they sicken now, little would save them; and some of the infants were already sick.

More than their constant pangs of hunger and discomfort, there was the fear of Indians. The land was, or had been, Indian land, and there was fear lest the Indians would return to take it back, despite the fact that Lewis Jones had insisted to the Argentine government that the Indians be compensated for the land the Welsh had been given. Garrisons and forts marked the line of scattered towns to the north of them, where Indians would descend on isolated houses or settlements, and kill the men and carry off the women and children. The Welsh had no firearms, except for the seventeen rifles issued at Liverpool and a limited quantity of ammunition. They had only a few work horses; and, in any case, did not know how to ride. They had no protection, and they knew themselves to be helpless should the Indians attack. Every twig that cracked, every spiral of dust seen in the distance, every yelp of a fox, they took to be signals of Indian scouts alerted to their presence. Every sudden fall of silence or cessation of birdsong threw them into panic. One day, they knew, the Indians would come. The only question was when.

Their only source of water, shared by man and beast alike, was diminishing and becoming contaminated. The site at New Bay was never intended to be permanent, and within a few days of them landing there, it was decided to move the settlement to the river, where the land was fertile and could sustain a colony.

While *Mimosa* remained anchored in the bay like a figurehead herself – the colony's guiding spirit – groups of men left New Bay at intervals, hoping to reach the Chubut valley, forty miles to the south. In the wild terrain, they became disoriented and lost their way. Some became separated from the group and from each other; and all suffered hunger and such raging thirst that many were reduced to drinking their own urine.

"I thought I would die of hunger and thirst there," William Jones of Bala later wrote to his uncle in Wales.

Thirteen days after their arrival, in the predawn hours, Elizabeth, the wife of Maurice Humpreys, gave birth to a girl, in the hut which he had roofed from the planks of wood dismantled from *Mimosa*'s berths. She was named Mary, after little Mary Jones, who had died on board on the day of landing. A range of hills in the area of New Bay is called Bryniau Meri, or Lomas María, after her.

She was the first Welsh baby to be born in Patagonia; and her birth gave them hope that, despite the difficulties that seemed insurmountable, they would survive in the new land to which they had come.

Departure from New Bay

Mimosa remained in New Bay for at least a month, possibly six weeks, to give time for the unloading of furniture and belongings. During that time, there were several more deaths.

Eight days after their arrival, seventeen-month-old Henry Hughes from Rhosllanerchrugog, the youngest of John and Elizabeth Hughes' four children, died. (Three months later, their four-year-old daughter, Myfanwy Mary, also died.) The day following little Henry Hughes' death, Margaret Anne, the fifteen-month-old child of Evan and Anne Davies, also died. She was their only child. Two weeks later, Catherine Davies, the mother of the hydrocephalic child who died on board, died and was buried in the dunes, leaving her widowed husband, Robert and their two young sons, William and Henry, to mourn for her.

For William and Catherine Jones of Bala tragedy struck again, when their only surviving daughter, Jane, died, probably of pneumonia. She was sixteen months old. Paradoxically, she was the last to be buried in New Bay, her little sister Mary being the first.

Why *Mimosa* remained for so long in New Bay is not known. It is only known that she did, under the orders of Michael D Jones to Pepperell.[38] As well as the time needed to unload her, it is possible that she sustained some damage during the seven-thousand-mile voyage that needed to be repaired. Certainly the dismantling of bunks, unloading of furniture and farm implements from the hold, and rowing them to the shore would have taken a couple of weeks or more, given the fact that the weather might not have been favourable every day and that many of the men who might have assisted the crew were either building enclosures for the livestock, or were attempting to find a way to the valley.

On September 7, one of the crew, twenty-year-old Francis Mitchell from Arbroath, in Scotland, deserted, indicating that *Mimosa* was still in

New Bay at that date, perhaps in readiness to depart. How he fared, or where he went, unless he had one of *Mimosa*'s lifeboats, is not known. The only place to which he could have gone was Carmen de Patagones, which he could have not have reached except by boat.

When *Mimosa*'s anchor was finally raised and her sails filled out in the wind, those watching her departure from the beach of New Bay must have experienced feelings akin to panic and loss. *Mimosa* was their last remaining contact with the outside world, with Wales and with their families there. Without *Mimosa* they were truly alone, isolated in the most desolate part of the world, without the means to leave it.

Homeward Bound

The precise date when *Mimosa* departed from New Bay is not known, but it was certainly either on, or a day or two after, Francis Mitchell's desertion. On October 24, *Mimosa* arrived at Maceió, in northeast Brazil, where the desertion of Francis Mitchell was reported to the British Vice-Consul.[39]

Mimosa arrived back in Liverpool on November 23, with a cargo of 2,623 baled bags of cotton in her hold, which she had loaded at Maceió. By December 13 of the same year, she was ready to depart from Liverpool again, ready for the next stage of her seagoing life – mainly carrying cotton from Maceió.

Part VI

Mainly Cotton

They buy cotton-wool in London that comes first from Cyprus and Smyrna, and at home work the same and perfect it into fustians, vermillions, dimities and other such stuffs and then return it to London where the same is vented and sold and not seldom sent into foreign parts.

Lewes Roberts, *Treasure of Traffic*

Cotton

Cotton, a word derived from its Arabic name, *qutun*, belonging to the *Gossypium* genus, has been cultivated since time immemorial. Cotton was grown, spun and woven into cloth in the Nile valley in Ancient Egypt; in the Indus valley; and, in pre–Aztec and pre-Inca times, in Mexico and Peru. In his travels in India in 484 BC, Herodotus made mention of the cotton garments worn there, and through the trade routes established by Alexander the Great, in his military conquests, cotton from India was brought overland and by boat by Arab merchants to Alexandria, from whence it was taken to North Africa, Persia, Turkey and Greece. The Romans began their own military conquests and adopted the use of cotton from their Egyptian provinces. Cotton clothing was a status symbol among Roman citizens, and a luxury which only the wealthiest could afford.

By the 9th century, Spain was the foremost country in Europe in the production of cotton textiles, which were being woven and dyed in Córdoba, Seville and Grenada, and cotton paper began to replace papyrus and linen. Renaissance Italy became the focus of artistic expression in clothing as well as in the arts and science, and Venice led the fashion in intricately dyed cotton clothing, as an alternative to old-fashioned armour and wool, and became the principal cotton city of the world.

In 1497, Vasco da Gama sailed from Lisbon, round the tip of Africa, to the city of Calicut in India, establishing a sea route by which an endless supply of Indian calico could be brought to Portugal, which replaced Venice as the main supplier of cotton goods to the world. A century later, the Netherlands assumed this role, from whence the knowledge of spinning cotton was taken to England in the second half of the 16th century, by Flemish weavers fleeing Spanish persecution, who settled in and around Manchester. Before this, cotton was used in England mainly for the manufacture of candlewicks. Wool woven for cloth and exported to Germany, Flanders and Russia, was the country's main source of wealth in textiles. In 1685, more than fifty-thousand Huguenots, driven out of France, settled in Spitalfields and introduced new methods of silk and cotton weaving. At the same time, English colonists started to grow cotton in their colonies in Virginia and the Carolinas.

The British East India Company, established in 1624, met the growing demand for cheap cotton goods in Britain by shipping cottons from India. Alarmed farmers and wool merchants lobbied Parliament to forbid the import of cotton textiles and even the wearing of cotton clothing. Efforts to legislate against the import of cotton failed, and despite high import tariffs and laws forbidding the inclusion of cotton in wool cloth, the tide of the rising cotton industry in England could not be turned back. Men preferred calico shirts to linen; women discarded woollen dresses and undergarments in favour of light muslins, cotton petticoats and 'bengals', as shawls from India were called. Woollen shrouds for the burial of the dead were abandoned in favour of cotton, and English fleeces lost some of their significance. In and around Manchester, cotton textile mills began to outnumber woollen mills. The fly shuttle, the spinning jenny, the water-powered spinning frame and, later, the power loom were invented before the 19th century.

Once, London was the chief cotton port of England. By the 19th century, because of its proximity to Manchester and the Lancashire cotton mills, Liverpool became the leading cotton port, not only in England, but in the world. Early in the 19th century, Liverpool importers and Manchester dealers traded through buying and selling brokers – one broker bought from the Liverpool importers, another sold to the Manchester dealers, who, in turn, sold to the spinners. Cotton futures, cotton clearing houses and cotton banks lay in the not too distant future.

Raw cotton, imported to Liverpool and spun and woven into cloth by the cotton mills in Lancashire, was re-exported to every known part of the world, in the form of shirting, calico, canvas, muslin, cretonne, lace, gauze, umbrella cloth, apron cloth, sail cloth, book-binding cloth, shroud cloth, butter cloth, brattice cloth for lining mine shafts, mosquito netting, blankets, towelling, bagging, lamp- and candle-wicks – the so-called Manchester goods – and the vast empire, stretching to every part of the globe, required cotton to clothe its soldiers.

By the end of the 19th century, cotton exported from Liverpool clothed one third of the human race.

The Cotton Cargoes

The *Gossypium brasiliensis* is indigenous to Brazil, and had been spun and woven into cloth by the Indians before the arrival of the Portuguese. By the end of the 18th century, the cotton-growing region comprised a two-hundred-mile belt in the northeast and a strip along the Sao Francisco valley. Until the cultivation of cotton in America, Brazil was the fourth largest cotton-producing country in the world and supplied one quarter of the supply consumed in Britain – the world's greatest consumer of raw cotton. With the development of the Lancashire cotton manufacture in the late eighteenth century, cotton exports from the northeastern Brazil increased rapidly and far outweighed the importance of coffee. (Only by the mid 19th century did coffee exports begin to overshadow those of cotton and sugar.) As with the sugar industry in Bahia and Pernambuco, cultivation of cotton grown in the northeast was reliant on slave labour. Known by the region in which it was grown – Maceió, Pernan (Pernambuco), Ceará – Brazilian cotton was especially well adapted for mixing with wool.

During the late 18th century, the West Indies produced 70% of the supply for Britain's still-young industry, and Brazil 8%, while the colonies in Virginia supplied less than 1%. So insignificant was the Virginian supply that when, in 1784, an American merchant resident in Liverpool imported a consignment of eight bags, it was confiscated by the port officials under the Cromwellian Navigation Law, on the premise that it could not have been grown in America and, therefore, the American vessel carrying it must have contravened the law. Even when it was released, the consignment lay in the warehouse until it rotted, there being no market for such a commodity. By the middle of the 19th century, America was the world's largest supplier.

Between 1780 and 1820, Brazil was one of the most important suppliers of raw cotton to the Lancashire mills. So great was Britain's need for raw cotton that Brazil could not supply all that was demanded, and between 1820 and 1860, raw cotton from America, India and Egypt exceeded the amount imported from Brazil.

During the American Civil War, between 1861 and 1865, supplies from America were cut off. The so-called 'cotton famine' was to Brazil's advantage, and cotton grown in the north eastern provinces of Pernambuco, Maranhao, Algoas (whose port was Maceió), Paraíba and Bahia, replaced sugar as Brazil's most important export. Cotton exports reached their peak in 1873, after which, although still an important export, they declined as coffee from Rio de Janeiro and Sao Paulo became the next boom. By the 1880s, falling prices on the Liverpool cotton exchange, the resumption of North American cotton production, and the abolition of slavery was, if not the death knell for Brazilian cotton-growers, a serious setback to the economy of the northeast.

It was calculated that a 200-ton ship could carry 58 tons of cargo. Cotton, being a light commodity, a ton of cotton took up three or four times as much space as a ton of sugar.

The bagged bales, each weighing from 200 to 300 lbs., were packed in the ship's hold in tiers. When no more bales could be forced in by hand, strong boards were inserted between the bales, screw jacks inserted between them, and the bales forcibly prised apart, to allow the insertion of yet more bales. The tightly screwed in bales so strained wooden hulled ships such as *Mimosa* that it was not unknown for such ships to break apart under the strain while at sea.

As well as her cargoes of cotton, *Mimosa* occasionally carried salted hides, isinglass (a form of gelatine derived from fish bladders); and, on her last but one voyage to Brazil, she carried a cargo of over 200 bags of cocoa for the cocoa king of Liverpool, J.S. Fry.

Last Voyages to Brazil

By December 13, 1865, *Mimosa* began the last of her Brazilian voyages. She was on her way back to Bahia. She took no more cargo to Rio de

Janeiro, and it is likely that She sailed in ballast. She was captained by George Pepperell, who was to have charge of her for the next five years; and four of those who had sailed on her during the voyage to Patagonia signed on again, including the mate, John Downes.

As with her previous voyages to Brazil, not one voyage was without incident. There were delays in sailing from Liverpool, caused by bad weather or when substitutes had to be found for crew who failed to come on board. Many of the crew were troublesome, some violent, refusing to sign the *Articles of Agreement* binding them to codes of behaviour while on board, and abusive to Pepperell and his officers. There were incidents of drunkenness, even among some of the stewards. Some of the crew were negligent during their watches, and fell asleep. One attacked Pepperell savagely with a knife, causing him the temporary loss of the use of his arm. Another attacked the mate on board with a sharp object, almost causing the mate the loss of an eye. There were desertions and discharges at the Brazilian ports, stowaways, complaints of alleged mistreatment against Pepperell, and deaths by drowning, when men fell overboard, all of which necessitated formal reports to the British consuls. Two of the crew contracted venereal diseases and had to be sent to a hospital in Pernambuco for treatment. One of these was Matthew Warren from St John, New Brunswick, who had sailed on *Mimosa* to Patagonia. Three and a half weeks after his return to duty, while *Mimosa* sailed back towards Liverpool, Matthew Warren was presumed dead. Pepperell documented the event in *Mimosa*'s log.

On Monday the 17th inst. at 4 A.M. ship running before a Gale from SSW and a heavy sea running and very dark. Matthew Warren was missed from the deck (and) some time had elapsed before it was found that he had fallen overboard ... There was not the slightest possibility of saving the poor fellow's life for the night was very dark, not a star visible, the sky overcast and the Ship running at the rate of 12 knots per hour and a heavy sea running. He must have been some distance astern even when the alarm was given, for some time had elapsed before our voice could have been understood amidst the noise of the storm.[40]

On January 5, 1869, *Mimosa* carried William Killey's twenty-year-old son, also called William Killey, who travelled on board as supercargo. It was his first voyage on *Mimosa*. Pepperell hoped that there would be no trouble with the crew on this voyage – with the owner's son on board.

Even before *Mimosa* sailed, Pepperell knew that this would not be the trouble-free voyage he had hoped for. Seven seamen, who had signed on, had not come on board at the allocated time, and riggers had to be employed to tow *Mimosa* to the Pier Head, involving additional expense. After the seamen boarded at the pier and *Mimosa* proceeded to sea, Pepperell discovered that, against regulations, all were wearing sheath knives. Clearly they would, and did, give trouble as the voyage proceeded. The weather grew worse, and *Mimosa* was not faring well. Young William Killey, an inexperienced sailor, and perhaps a seasick one, must have feared for his life as *Mimosa* shuddered and rolled in the rough seas encountered in St George's Channel. The crew accommodation was deluged, rendering it uninhabitable, until the carpenter had repaired and caulked it, and three weeks off Bahia, a leak in one of the water tanks caused a severe shortage of water.

Perhaps young William Killey's report to his father on conditions on board was less than favourable, for it was after that, at the end of 1870, when William Killey decided that the time had come to be rid of *Mimosa*.

Towards an End to an Era

The clipper ship era was coming to an end, the ships were becoming uneconomic: they cost too much to build, repair and maintain, required too many hands to sail them, and they wore out too soon. Designed for speed, their lines were too slim to carry much cargo. Insurance costs, too, were high, as were interest and depreciation, wages, pilotage, costs of loading and dispatching, disbursements at ports like Anjer, Shanghai, Rio de Janeiro, Pernambuco and Maceió. Oak forests in England and Scotland were being seriously depleted, after centuries of vigorous shipbuilding, and import duties on foreign-grown timber were prohibitive. Iron ships were less costly to build and maintain, if considerably less aesthetic.

By the latter half of the 19th century, the end of the working sailing ship was in sight, and in the fierce scramble for cargoes, the clipper was being squeezed out. The only cargoes that paid were large ones, and the clipper ship, for all its speed, was never designed to carry large cargoes. Besides, there was talk of a canal being built from the Red Sea into the Mediterranean, to eliminate the necessity of going around the Cape of Good Hope. More ominously, smoke-belching steamships were making the voyage to Australia, China and South America more economically than clippers.

The future for *Mimosa* was not a bright one. She might follow the fate of other once-proud clippers and become a freighter, tramping from port to port in search of any cargo she could get. She might be pounded to pieces on some reef, or go down with all hands in a storm; it was a miracle that she had, so far, survived such a fate. She might suffer the ultimate humiliation for a clipper, of being dismasted and used as a coaling barge for the steamships now ruling the seas, whose proliferation sounded the death knell for her and her stately sisters.

At this point, it must have crossed William Killey's mind that, from now on, the cost of repairs would increase, especially when *Mimosa* reached the end of her classification and would have to be reclassified. She was no longer profitable. She was becoming a liability rather than an asset, and William Killey began to consider divesting himself of her while he could.

The Last Transactions

Mimosa returned from her voyage to Bahia on July 16, 1869, and William Killey decided to sell *Mimosa,* while he could still get a fair price for her.

The heady days of the 1850s, when Britain's commercial supremacy in Brazil was unrivalled, were changing. As Brazil came of age throughout the latter part of the 19th century, there was increasing resentment of the influence and control Britain exerted over its economy. Other nations, like America and Germany, were challenging Britain's monopoly, causing prudent shipowners like William Killey to look elsewhere for markets. In her early voyages to Brazil, he had no trouble in getting orders for all the sugar or cotton *Mimosa* could carry. Now, he had difficulty in obtaining sufficient orders to fill her hold, and she frequently sailed to Brazil in ballast.

Moreover, because of her voyage to Patagonia, *Mimosa* was gaining an unwelcome notoriety. First, there were the deaths of children on the outward-bound passage, followed by more deaths on land. Letters in the Liverpool newspapers, one of which was based on an account from the young doctor, who, presumably, could not be suspected of being prone to exaggeration, appeared to confirm the rumours that the colony was on the verge of collapse, and *Mimosa*'s name was being documented in government correspondence. It had not done the reputation of Killey & Co., as the company had been called three years after the voyage to Patagonia, any good to have been identified with such a harebrained scheme. Even though the ship had been chartered, the Vining & Killey name was still associated with it, since they were the owners.

Mimosa was becoming a liability – more than that, an embarrassment – of which William Killey wished to rid himself. Four years had passed since her last survey, and he wished to avoid the cost of another. *Mimosa*'s hull was sound, for the stately Glen Tanar oak had withstood well the battering of almost two decades at sea. She would last a few more years yet, but not many.

The partnership of owners was such that getting everyone's agreement on what to do with her would be tiresome and time-consuming. William Killey knew enough about committees to know that there would always be one dissenting voice overriding his own. Some of the original shareholders had died and their shares had been bought or inherited by others. Robert Vining was aging, and showed less and less interest in shipping and more in his civic commitments. William Killey decided, therefore, to act on his own.

Mimosa, homeward bound from Bahia, returned to Liverpool on April 9, 1870. Seemingly unknown to William Killey, on March 4, 1870, Trevanion Hugo's heir, Thomas, a ship's chandler in Liverpool, and his partner, James Hughes, a plumber, also of Liverpool, sold their 4 shares in *Mimosa* to John Gray, a master mariner, or retired master mariner, living in London. Perhaps annoyed that the shares had not been offered first to him, William Killey decided his course of action.

One by one, William Killey met with or wrote to all *Mimosa*'s shareholders. He pointed out the difficulty of obtaining freight for her and asserted that there was no hope of chartering her as an emigrant ship again, for he did not foresee a another group as desperate or as foolhardy as the Welsh, willing to charter a ship as old as *Mimosa*. One by one, he made his offers; and one by one, the offers were accepted.

On November 30, 1870, just three weeks after *Mimosa* returned from what was to be her last voyage to Brazil and her last voyage under George Pepperell, Charles Wigg and Henry William Eddis, a merchant and an accountant, both from Liverpool, sold the 8 shares they held under mortgage for £282 from Eliza Hamilton of Notting Hill, London, who evidently was unable to pay back her loan.

On December 2, Emma Wood, the widow of John Wood of Glossop in Derby, sold the 16 shares she had inherited from her husband. On December 30, John Broadbent Wood, a merchant of Carr, sold the 8 shares he had inherited the year before from John Broadbent, who was possibly his uncle.

The New Year dawned. *Mimosa* lay in dock, while her fate was being decided. No cargo was sought, no voyage planned, no crew signed on. It is certain that, by then, William Killey had an interested buyer.

On January 30, 1871, Daniel Green and Richard Green, respectively, relinquished their 8 and 4 shares. Daniel Green was now sixty-five and had been retired since his last ship, *Kensington*, while on the East Indies run, had been lost at sea five years before. For him, as well as for *Mimosa*, it was an end to an era. He had been *Mimosa*'s designated master, while she was being constructed. Undoubtedly, he inspected the half-model of her hull, perhaps suggesting modifications to be implemented by William Hall. He had been a part-owner since the beginning of *Mimosa*'s seagoing life. It is impossible that he would not have felt saddened that the clipper he had known since its conception was now to be put up for sale.

Together with the 16 shares which he held jointly with Robert Vining, William Killey owned 60 shares, while John Gray stubbornly held onto his 4. William Killey was running out of patience. Based on a letter to Robert Vining, written in 1884, the year before Robert Vining's death, recommending sale of their barque, *Bella*, William Killey's communication to him would have read as follows:

Dear Sir,

The barque Mimosa of which you hold 4 /64ths shares is at Liverpool from Bahia in Brazil. Seeing that the vessel is 18 years old and is in consequence of her size and age unable to compete profitably with vessels of more modern type, we as owners of considerably more than half the vessel consider it desirable to sell her and shall feel obliged if you will advise us of your concurrence in this step.

We are, Dear Sir,

Yours faithfully,

William Killey.

On February 8, John Gray agreed to sell his 4 shares. Now it just remained for William Killey to persuade his former partner to relinquish the shares they jointly held.

Finally, on February 15, 1871, William Killey bought out Robert Vining, by acquiring all 16 shares that they held jointly, making him sole owner of *Mimosa*.

The following day, he sold her to Peter Stuart and Peter Douglas, two of the largest Liverpool traders in West African palm oil in, who each purchased 32 shares, making them equal owners.

Part VII

Last Port of Call

There is not another tree in the whole world which produces money with so little expense as this particular crop.

E D Morel, *Affairs of West Africa*

Palm Oil

In its natural habitat, the *elaesis guineensis*, from which palm oil is produced, grows along the labyrinthine rivers and creeks of the Niger delta in the Gulf of Guinea, in West Africa. In the 19th century, there were five main ports on the delta coast that traded in palm oil: Old Calabar, Bonny, Brass, New Calabar and Opobo. Old Calabar, called Calabarra by the Portuguese, who traded in spices, ivory and slaves, lies on the west bank of the Calabar river, which, with the Cross river, forms an estuary twelve miles wide at its mouth and fifty in length. A slave port for two centuries, from 1650 until 1841, it became the leading trading port in palm oil, the capital of the 'oil rivers' of the malaria-infested Niger delta, and the headquarters of European administration in the delta before Lagos. Brass, on the Brass River, east of the main channel of the river, is named from the brass that was bartered for slaves and palm oil. Bonny, on the river of the same name, had, from the 15th century, gained its wealth from the slave trade. New Calabar lay a hundred and twenty miles to the west, near Bonny, deeper into the delta area, on the Kalabari or 'New' Calabar river.

Opobo was established, when one of the kings of Bonny broke away, to form a rival settlement.

Three distinct zones run parallel to the coast into which the 'oil' rivers flow: the delta itself, the forest region and the plateau region. Fringed with immense mangrove forests, the mosquito-infested delta region is swampy, with a network of creeks, wooded islands and broad, sluggish channels carpeted with gigantic water lilies. In times of flood, the waters rise up and spread over the land, drowning some of the islands. The climate is humid because of heavy rainfall, hot and extremely unhealthy. Great tropical trees covered with creepers line the banks, their branches sometimes interlacing above to form a canopy.

North of the delta, the mangroves disappear and the land rises, gradually at first, then becoming hilly, and is covered with dense and abundant concentrations of *elaesis guineensis*. Beyond the forests of palm, the land becomes undulating, with isolated table mountains of granite and sandstone rising abruptly from the plains to form a plateau cloaked with acacias, feathery mimosas and tamarinds: and it forms part of the great plateau of North Africa.

One palm bears fruit after its fourth year of growth, producing one hundred gallons of oil each year, and bears fruit for at least sixty years. The harvest, which begins after the start of the rainy season in late February, was regulated by the tribal elders. The clusters of nuts were cut from the tree, either with a knife attached to a long bamboo pole, or by a climber, who would be attached to the trunk by a raffia fibre rope. Windfalls were collected from the ground. The collected nuts were stored in vast pits or upturned canoes covered with palm fronds, and left to ferment. They were then boiled in water, and pounded in mortars, to remove the fleshy pericarp from the kernel. The pulp was boiled again, after which, the released oil was skimmed. Finally, the pots of oil were canoed through the maze of creeks and waterways to the port, or head-loaded through the forests, hills and mangrove swamps to Old Calabar, Bonny and the other former slave ports.

Palm oil, which became so important and valuable a commodity in Britain in the 19th century, had been known for tens of thousands of years, but was of little interest to the traders making fortunes from the slave trade. With the abolition of the slave trade, Liverpool merchants with slave trading links in West Africa turned their attention to the palm oil, hitherto bought only to feed their slaves on the sea voyages to the Caribbean. The former Liverpool slavers knew the West Africa run. They knew the rivalries of the African kings who controlled the rivers, the native pilots and the middlemen, and were attuned to tribal customs. Their links with West Africa were already in place and well-established. Trade in one commodity was changed to trade in another. The transition was as smooth as the oil itself, and Liverpool emerged as the major centre for West African palm oil. Despite London's attempts to break into the trade and competition from Bristol, the delta remained the preserve of Liverpool traders. Liverpool became the foremost port for the import of palm oil in Britain and the world.

In the 19th century, palm oil was used by every household in Britain. Their rooms were lit by candles made from it. They washed themselves and their clothes with soap made from it, and spread the margarine made from the kernels on their bread, while tinplate using palm oil in its manufacture canned their food. The textile industry required oils for wool, and soap for the cotton and calico industry. Trams and trains, whose wheels and engines were greased with palm oil, carried them on their journeys or to the factories where they worked the machinery driving Britain's economy, which was lubricated with it; and if they were sick, their doctors sometimes prescribed medicine containing glycerine, a refined by-product of palm oil.

Depending on the fatty acid content, palm oil was broadly defined into two categories: 'soft' oil and 'hard' oil. Soft oil was low in fatty acids and was used in soap manufacture, machine lubrication and tinplate processing. Hard oil, high in fatty acid content, was used in candle manufacture and for certain kinds of soap.

Competition for the lucrative profits was intense. From 1810, prices in palm oil rose steadily, with sharp increases in the decade from 1820 to 1830. During the period from the late 1830s to the early 1840s, there was a levelling off of prices, with a slight decline in the late 1840s. Prices rose to dizzying heights in the 1850s – the golden years of the palm oil trade – reaching a peak in 1854. As in the gold rush days in California and Australia, others from Liverpool, London and beyond were eager to make such apparently easy fortunes as those enjoyed by the 'oilearchy', not realizing the risks involved. Technological advances in the making of soap and lubricants began to replace the need for palm oil; and the greater use of electricity and decline in demand for candles, and the emergence of other sources of *elaesis guineensis* in Southeast Asia and Malaysia decreased the demand for West African oil. In 1862, prices plunged, and many of the established traders went bankrupt, or decided to cut their losses. By 1864, only three Liverpool firms were trading in the delta area. One of these was Stuart & Douglas.

The Two Peters

Peter Stuart was born in Liverpool in 1814. His father, also called Peter, came from an English mercantile family in Genoa, where he was born, settling in Liverpool after serving under Nelson at the Battle of Trafalgar. He established himself as a master carpenter and was the owner of a prosperous cooperage business, which he intended to hand over to his son. Peter Stuart senior wished his son to learn every aspect of it, so that he might become a master cooper; and when he was a young man, Peter Stuart was apprenticed to the cooperage trade.

In the years of his apprenticeship, young Peter Stuart learned to split by hand long logs of oak into staves that were left to season from one to five years. In a brick shed, he learned the skill of shaping the staves to make barrels and casks that could be shipped, either assembled or dismantled, to every part of the world. Held together with iron hoops, the man-high casks had to be watertight and bear the strain of transportation. He learned how a newly-made cask, quarter-filled with boiling water and rolled around, would show faults in workmanship by the tell-tale escape of steam. He learned how to sound with a mallet a barrel unloaded from a ship's hold in order to detect the amount of leakage from the level of its contents, and to inspect the bilge water for excess amounts of leakages. Sometimes leakage occurred through a worm hole in the wood, and he learned to enlarge the cavity and hammer in a wooden spike, which, sawn off level with the outside of the cask, would be hardly visible. Under a master cooper, he learned that the true test of a well-made cask was how it fared during loading, rough-handling and transportation.

Oak casks and barrels were required for almost every trade with which Liverpool was associated, and were in high demand. At twenty-six, Peter Stuart became head of the largest cooperage business in Liverpool. In time, it covered over four acres and was the most efficiently-run cooperage business in Europe.

Like his brothers and sisters, Peter Stuart spoke Italian fluently. He was an intimate friend of Garibaldi and Mazzini, who was godfather to one of his sons, and he was a supporter of Italian Unification. Peter Stuart was a staunch Liberal and a firm believer in the independence of nation states. Using his wealth, he gave ships to Garibaldi to aid Italian

Unification, and assisted Hungarian refugees fleeing the oppression of the Austro-Hungarian Empire. He believed passionately in justice, without regard to class or position, fought vigorously for the abolition of the Corn Laws, and held the conviction that there would be no peace in Europe until monarchies disappeared.

He studied phrenology and homeopathic medicine, becoming a devotee and friend of the founder of homeopathy, Dr Samuel Hahnemann. For forty years, he dispensed treatments freely to the sick-poor who sought them, which put him at odds with traditional physicians who were not inclined to give consultations on the same non-monetary basis. An admirer of the Hebrew scholar, John Bellamy, he learned Hebrew himself, so that he could have a better understanding of the books of the Old Testament.

He married Ellen Moss, who was Paris-educated and a brilliant pianist. She felt as strongly as he did that their children should know French, Italian and German, as well as English, so that they would be as much at home at home in Continental Europe as they were in England. Her brother, Henry Moss, was the founder of the Liverpool ship-broking firm, H E Moss & Co. When first married, Peter and Ellen Stuart lived in a residential district of Liverpool for people of moderate means. As their family and wealth increased, they moved to Farnworth, from where Peter Stuart travelled into Liverpool by dog-cart. Finally, in 1861, he purchased Elm House, in Seaforth, a mansion in the heart of the country, surrounded by open fields. They had nine children: two daughters, born first, and seven sons.

In his book, *The Life of Peter Stuart*, his biographer, Larry Finigan, says of his subject that:

Whether in medicine, science, politics or business he was a revolutionary ... He fought for what he believed and believed (in) what he fought for. He had that rare combination, the mind of a thinker as well as that of a man of action.

★

The young man, who had travelled as supercargo on board the ship anchored in one of the oil rivers of the Niger delta, mopped his perspiring face as he paced the deck, scanning the banks for some sign of human life. Crocodiles reclined on mud banks. Buffalo and hippos wallowed in the creeks. Parrots flew in raucous flocks. Jewel-breasted kingfishers and yellow palm birds flitted above the water. Ruins of barracoons, where penned slaves once awaited shipment, bore silent witness to a trade that brought riches and shame in equal measure to its perpetrators. The stifling, miasma-laden air of the delta pressed upon him so heavily that he sometimes found it difficult to breathe, let alone work, and swarms of mosquitoes assailed him in high-pitched, whining clouds.

Finally, after he had been there for almost a month, a canoe manned by forty paddlers emerged from one of the countless creeks hidden by dense vegetation and made its way towards the ship. After climbing on board, the native trader, with signs and gestures, promised to deliver a sufficient quantity of palm oil to complete the ship's cargo, in return for an advance payment to enable him to collect it. The days passed; month followed month without the promised delivery of palm oil. One by one, the crew became stricken with malaria and not a few died. The supercargo checked the amount of palm oil that was eventually delivered, and calculated the net profit to his employer in Liverpool. Give or take a percentage or two, the profit would amount to 300%. The name of the supercargo was Peter Douglas.

Peter Douglas, also from Liverpool, was a doctor by profession, who, as a young man, in the 1830s, had been in the employ of G A & W Maxwell & Co., one of the leading palm oil traders in Liverpool, serving first as a ship's doctor on board the Maxwell's ships sailing to West Africa, and later as supercargo.

At one time, Maxwell & Co. had dealt through the masters of their ships, who were given all discretionary powers to trade for oil, which frequently involved voyages lasting a year or more. Yellow fever, malaria and desertions reduced crews. Some of the ships' masters, like their crews, were brutal, foul-tempered drunkards. Sheer boredom was endemic and was alleviated only by visits to the sailors' drinking dens and brothels, on the island of Fernando Po. Eventually, it became expedient for firms like Maxwell & Co. to replace their ships' masters with supercargoes. With a supercargo employed, the ship's master could return to Liverpool with another of Maxwell's' ships that was already loaded with oil, leaving the supercargo on board the incoming ship to trade and await the next consignment.

The first time that Peter Douglas saw the surf breaking on the blindingly white sands of the coast of West Africa, he had been a young man in his twenties. From the deck of the ship – one of the many which Maxwell & Co. owned – he saw the long, grey levels of mangroves, and caught the pungent aroma of heat and tropical vegetation that emanated from the coasts that were forever associated with the trades that gave them their names: the Ivory Coast, the Gold Coast, and the Slave Coast.

Although Peter Douglas was employed, not now as a doctor, but as a supercargo, his medical training made him cognisant of the medical conditions that prevailed on the oil rivers. The delta was one of the unhealthiest places in the world, meriting the description 'white man's grave'. Malaria, cholera, dengue and yellow fever routinely cut swathes through the population, black and white. Dysentery, caused by drinking the fly- and amoeba-infected waters of the creeks and rivers, was frequently fatal. Bilharzias, a parasitic-borne infection contracted by bathing in or drinking infected water, affected the mucus membrane of the urinary passages, bladder and kidneys, resulting in urinary calculi and endemic haematuria and anaemia through loss of blood. Thermic fever, or siriasis, commonly known as sunstroke, also took its victims. Leprosy, too, was prevalent.

As well as the endemic diseases, there was the season of the dreaded 'smokes', when the hot, dry *harmattan* wind brought a thick haze of red dust that darkened the air of the delta coast. While the parching wind blew, during December, January and February, enveloping the whole area in dense fog, the Africans smeared their bodies with oil or fat to guard against its desiccating effects, while the Europeans on board ships anchored in the estuaries tried to repel the vapour they believed to be injurious to their health by fumigating their vessels by burning tobacco leaves.

For most European traders, including him, return to Liverpool could not come fast enough. Trading, he observed, was long and laborious. Practices that had evolved in the slave trade era continued unchanged, except for the nature of the merchandise; the master of the ship, or, if there was one, the supercargo, negotiating exchange of goods before returning with all speed to Liverpool. Since Europeans were not permitted to reside on shore or to establish bases upriver, trading was done on board ship. Certain ceremonies had to be observed; nothing could be rushed. Goods brought from Liverpool, like salt and cloth, were given to African middlemen acting on behalf of their kings, on credit or trust, in exchange for oil. (Salt, of which Liverpool had abundance, was once so precious that 12th century African and Arab traders exchanged it for twice its weight in gold.)

Trust being established, without which trading was impossible, fleets of hundreds of canoes set out for the interior. The harvest, which began after the start of the rainy season, in late February, was regulated by the tribal elders; and it sometimes took months of tedium and boredom, if not a year or even two years, for the trust to be redeemed in the agreed quantities of oil.

As well as the payment of goods on credit, it was customary to give a 'dash' or a tip to keep the local king or chief's goodwill. In addition, 'comey', in the form of a customs duty and calculated on the carrying capacity of a vessel, was paid to the king for the privilege of trading. It was only after the payment of these dues that trading could commence.

Risking malaria, Peter Douglas travelled up the oil rivers and creeks, to see the oil markets of the interior. He saw the immense forests of palms and the enormous clusters of fruit that each tree bore. He saw how they were cut, fermented and pounded. He saw the amount of oil that each palm produced. He saw the urns of oil being loaded onto fleets of canoes, each canoe requiring as many as forty paddlers and carrying eight or nine tons of oil, to be transported to the former slave ports of Old Calabar and Bonny for shipment to Liverpool. Slavery, he saw, was by no means abolished in West Africa, where it had existed for centuries. The Portuguese were still shipping slaves to Bahia and the Caribbean, and the Africans and Arabs were still supplying them, unwilling to relinquish so lucrative and well-established a trade. As well, slaves were used in the labour-intensive production of palm oil and its transportation to the ships that awaited it. He observed that Europeans like himself and the masters and crews of Liverpool ships were held in low esteem by the Africans. (Few masters and supercargoes, in his opinion, treated the Africans with respect.) He saw the profits that were being made by African middlemen and the ships' masters and supercargoes. Especially, he observed the enormous profits that Maxwell & Co. made from each shipload of palm oil.

Unlike some of the other Liverpool firms trading in West Africa, Maxwell & Co. had not previously been involved in the slave trade.

Established in 1808, the brothers had been general merchants and had been involved in the palm oil trade only since 1830. Like every other firm operating in the delta, Maxwell & Co. was family-owned and admitted none except relatives or in-laws to the higher echelons of the business. Peter Douglas quickly saw that a future with them would always be limited to that of employee. Unless he married a Maxwell daughter, he would never share in the profits that enabled the brothers and their families, if they wished, to live like princes in Liverpool.

The trade was growing as demand in Britain for palm oil increased. New ideas were evolving. The founders of old established family firms were reaching retirement. New, energetic men, unrelated to one another, were forming companies and moving in. Peter Douglas began to think of trading on his own behalf. He had first-hand knowledge of the delta. He knew the risks involved. He knew some of the African middlemen and traders and, what was more important, they knew him. All one needed, he decided, was access to a limitless supply of casks, a reliable agent who would trade fairly with the Africans, and a partnership with someone of limitless vision willing to take a risk to buy or charter a ship to send to the delta.

Stuart & Douglas

A shrewd businessman as well as a philanthropic one, Peter Stuart kept a tally of the quantities of casks and barrels required by Liverpool traders exporting palm oil from Calabar to Liverpool, and observed that the tally, already large, was steadily rising. He knew little about West Africa, except in relation to the heinous slave trade which he abhorred, and he was well aware of the furore that abolition of slavery had caused among Liverpool merchants, who had grown rich from the trade in human flesh. Palm oil was in great demand at this time, and if the quantity of orders for casks was any indication, merchants hitherto associated with slavery were now trading just as lucratively in palm oil.

While still in his twenties, Peter Stuart was ready for a new challenge. He studied maps of West Africa, acquainted himself with the names of the men who traded there, and entered into one or two shipping transactions, which gave him practical insight into trading possibilities. In the course of his dealings, he met and made friends with a young man, also named Peter, who had an extensive knowledge of West Africa and of the trade that was reaping such enormous profits. Finally, in 1845, when Peter Stuart was thirty-one, the partnership of Stuart & Douglas was formed.

Two years later, Stuart & Douglas established themselves on the Brass River, by purchasing a small 282-ton barque and despatching it there. This was the Yarmouth-built *Adriana*, despatched under an agent, who had been instructed to promise the local African chiefs a share of the profits, on condition that they gave up the trade in slaves. *Adriana* was followed by *Woodpecker*, which sank on the homeward journey. An 816-ton, Quebec-built ship, *Jemima*, was purchased and sent to Bonny in 1848, followed by the 647-ton *Rothschild*.

Having established themselves on the Brass and Bonny, Stuart & Douglas decided to expand into New Calabar, where they had been trading from Bonny, and, in 1851, a 387-ton vessel, *Heroine*, was sent to New Calabar, to work the port as a separate agency. Four years after New Calabar had been established, Stuart & Douglas expanded their operations into Old Calabar, and, in 1855, they purchased a new iron vessel of 1,388 tons, which they named *Ellen Stuart*. She caused a sensation, being the largest vessel ever to trade in the oil rivers up to that time. She proved to be too large and uneconomical for the West African trade, however, and was placed on other trade routes that Stuart & Douglas had now established.

There seemed to be no limit to their success. Opobo was opened as a result of a quarrel among two rival chiefs, one breaking away from the Bonny River, and Stuart & Douglas were the first to trade there. A further opening was made at Lagos, but had to be abandoned.

Stuart & Douglas also had shipping interests in the Caribbean, the East Indian and Australian routes. (In lieu of a debt, Peter Stuart was offered the land on which Melbourne now stands, an offer he unfortunately decided not to accept.) Their vessel, *Stuart Hahnemann*, was lost on her maiden voyage, in the spring of 1875, while returning from Bombay. *Peter Stuart* and *Phrenologist* fared better. The barque *Royal Arch* once reached Barbados with a cargo of ivory, ebony, coffee and peanuts, with the master in irons, the crew having mutinied when he threatened to shoot them.

Ten years after its formation, Stuart & Douglas was the second largest palm oil trading company in Liverpool, with six factories on the delta. Mangroves were cut to lay roads, and coasting vessels and steam launches made the journeys to upriver markets more efficiently than canoes.

In 1889, Stuart & Douglas, facing falling prices for palm oil, and fierce competition from other Liverpool traders and the Africans themselves who could now ship their oil directly to Liverpool, London or Bristol in steamships, amalgamated with eight of the largest oil trading companies on the delta to form the African Association Ltd. of Liverpool. Its creation marked an end to an era, as it prevented any young Peters dreaming of emulating on the West African delta, what the old Peters had accomplished.

Voyage to New Calabar

In 1871, when Stuart & Douglas acquired *Mimosa*, she was eighteen years old. *Leichardt*, built in the Hall shipyard in 1853, was sunk on a voyage to New Zealand. *Hannibal* was wrecked on the run to China from Sydney, on its second voyage. *Chrysolite* was wrecked in a hurricane off Mauritius. *North Star* came to grief on the Pratas Shoal, when bound for Foochow from Hong Kong. Robert Vining's speedy *Reindeer* was lost on a coral reef off the coast of New South Wales. *John Taylor*, after passing through the Sunda Strait on the homeward voyage to Liverpool from Shanghai, was never heard of again. The splendid *Cairngorm* was wrecked on the River Min, while trying to navigate the treacherous Mingan Pass to the Pagoda Anchorage.

By 1871, *Mimosa* was an old lady, whose past was decidedly more romantic than her present. Her ribs creaked; her movements were slower. She stank of black bilge water and old age, and she leaked. She would not be able to stand many more storms, if any, and was fast approaching the time of being put into retirement. Soon, she would rest in her last mooring until she died of old age. Painted white, like all the Stuart & Douglas ships, *Mimosa* began to resemble a ghost.

She looked quaint and old-fashioned, with her acres of sails bleached white by salt and sun, like a white-haired old lady who had outlived most of her contemporaries, and for whom the modern age, with its speed and efficiency, lacked the romanticism of her youth. Vigorous, smoke-belching steamships now ruled the waves and made the journeys to China, Australia or South America faster, cheaper and more efficiently than *Mimosa* and her ethereally-beautiful sisters, although, in her element, on the ocean, in a brisk breeze that did not threaten to overpower her, she could still surprise herself by attaining a sudden burst of speed.

On March 18, 1871, *Mimosa* was ready for what was to become her final destination: New Calabar. Captaining her was a fifty-eight-year-old man called Stephen Goodman, who had taken ships to the West Indies and South Africa. Like *Mimosa* herself, he was nearing the end of his seagoing life on the unhealthy West African run, after sailing various

Stuart & Douglas ships for ten years.

On the night of the 20th, passing the Pembrokeshire coast as she headed down St George's Channel in poor visibility, *Mimosa* collided with an American ship, *Lepanto*, bound for Galveston from Newport.[41] Such was the damage to *Lepanto* that the poop, mizzen-head, rails, stanchions and masts were smashed, and the sails and yards were lost. Although she, too, had sustained damage and was leaking badly, *Mimosa* took the captain and crew of the *Lepanto* to Milford Haven. The incident was reported as follows:

Milford, 22nd March.

The Lepanto, reported yesterday as coming in with loss of mizzenhead, etc., arrived here during the night. She had been in collision on the night of the 20th March with a barque, when the master and part of the crew of the Lepanto got on board the barque. The Lepanto is bound from Newport to Galveston.

Mimosa lost an anchor and a cable. Alarmingly, she began to fill with water. Unable to proceed to sea, she returned to Liverpool to make repairs, and arrived two days later, on March 24.

Liverpool, 24 March.

The Mimosa bound for New Calabar which put back here, 22nd March, after collision, was docked yesterday. Her bows were severely injured, the foreyard and jib boom carried away, and she lost an anchor and cable. She made about half an inch more water per hour than usual after the accident.[42]

Stephen Goodman evidently possessed neither Pepperell's attention to detail nor his skill as a master, for *Mimosa*'s log makes no mention of the collision or gives any details of the voyage. Compulsory pilotage was abolished in 1871, and it is possible that Stephen Goodman had decided to dispense with one, so saving the cost.

What is known from the *Agreement and Account of Crew* is that *Mimosa* reached New Calabar by June, when several of the crew transferred to another of Stuart & Douglas's ships, *George Washington,* lying at Bonny. By July, Stephen Goodman had been relieved of his duties, possibly because of illness, or plain bad navigation, for he proceeded to Bonny, to sail back to Liverpool as a passenger on the *George Washington.*

For six months or more, *Mimosa* lay at New Calabar, being loaded with casks of palm oil, and manned by a skeleton crew that was augmented by native labour. A number was painted on each cask head and the amount of oil recorded. The casks were rolled into position and placed lengthwise, bung holes uppermost, on a bed of sand or shell, tier upon tier, the largest and strongest casks on the lowest tier to bear the weight of the casks on the upper tiers. The centre of her hold was filled first, and pieces of raffia were wedged between the casks to prevent them rubbing against one another in the voyage. After the first tier was in place, the next tier of casks was lashed into position to prevent rolling. During the voyage, the carpenter would check for leakages, and the casks would be hosed with sea water to rid *Mimosa*'s hold of the rancid smell of leaking oil.

In November, one of the seamen, a twenty-two-year-old man from Newfoundland, died of one of the many diseases endemic in the delta. He was buried on the evening of the same day, on the appropriately-named Snake Island.

On December 14, when *Mimosa* was ready to sail back to Liverpool, a master to replace Stephen Goodman came on board, along with eight crew, who had all been transferred from yet another of Stuart & Douglas's ships, *Royal Arch. Mimosa*'s new master was John Campbell, a sixty-year-old man from Jamaica who, like his predecessor, had spent the last ten years in Stuart & Douglas's service. He was *Mimosa*'s last known master.

To avoid the strong Guinea current and laborious beating against the prevailing winds, John Campbell would have sailed *Mimosa* south, to catch the S E Trade Winds, which would have enabled her to call at the island of Fernando Po, a regular point of departure for ships leaving the delta, where she could collect provisions and water for the journey back to Liverpool. Little of note appeared to have occurred during the voyage back to Liverpool, except that one of the crew died at sea. *Mimosa* arrived back in Liverpool on March 13, 1872, carrying 500 barrels of palm oil.

MIMOSA, @ NEW CALABAR
Dec 25, of L'pool, J Campbell, 15 m, 409 t
Stuart & Douglas, Q D
500 cks palm oil   Stuart & Douglas

Mimosa's *last cargo*

Liverpool Farewell

On May 11, 1872, *Mimosa* was ready to depart from Liverpool, with John Campbell at the helm. It was to be her last voyage and her final farewell to Liverpool. For the last time, ropes secured her to a tug, which bore her into the Mersey, and she sailed past the familiar landmarks, into St George's Channel and the open sea. This time there would be no return to Liverpool.

It was an uneventful voyage. There were no collisions; there were no deaths at sea, no men clapped in irons for misbehaviour. By June 28, she was in port at Bonny and remained there until after July 2. She reached New Calabar in July, and eight of the crew transferred to another ship. In October, John Campbell and the remainder of the crew were formally discharged, leaving *Mimosa* at New Calabar.

After October 1872, there is no record of other voyages. It is likely that, because of her size, she was used as a coasting vessel, sailing to the upriver markets to collect the casks of palm oil for Stuart & Douglas's ships at Bonny, Old and New Calabar. Again, because of her size, she would be able to cross the treacherous bars that lay across many of the rivers of the delta, which the larger sailing ships and steamships could not navigate. (The *Royal Arch* was wrecked on the New Calabar River in 1872. Another had been lost in the Bonny River in 1867; and another in the Brass River three years before.)

In 1875, *Mimosa* was listed for the first time in *Lloyd's Register of Shipping*,[43] when she would again have undergone a survey. She was found to be fit for the conveyance of dry and perishable goods to and from all parts of the world. Classifying and registering her at *Lloyd's* would have enabled Stuart & Douglas to get insurance for the goods she carried, as her classification guaranteed that her hull was watertight and her cargo safe from damp. The fact that Stuart & Douglas considered it worth the trouble and expense of the survey necessary for registration signified that *Mimosa* continued coasting along the rivers of the delta, calling at Stuart & Douglas's many trading depots. In so speculative and competitive a business, insurance was imperative by the 1870s. In 1879, she dropped out of the register and, on January 27, 1880, it is recorded that *Mimosa* was converted to a hulk.

The Hulk

'Hulk', from the Saxon word *hulc*, or possibly from the Greek word *holkas*, meaning a towed boat, was the word used for the body of a ship. In China, hulks were used as storage places for opium; and hulks were hidden on beaches the world over, wherever smuggling was rife. In 17th and 18th centuries, hulks of warships or East Indiamen, were used as prisons for convicts or rebels, like the captured Jacobites after Culloden, while awaiting transportation to the American colonies. Moored in the middle of wide swamps or in inaccessible stretches of the Thames, there was little possibility for escape. Men were kept shackled by the ankles, and hulk fever carried off·large numbers. By the late 1770s, transportation as a punishment was being questioned, as many who were sent as prisoners to the American colonies elected to remain there. after their prison sentences were completed, attaining varying measures of prosperity. After the American Revolution, Britain lost its main dumping ground for undesirables, and hulks became permanent floating jails and remained so until the system of transportation resumed, this time to Australia. They were finally abolished in 1867.

Ships that had been specially converted to hulks to serve a specific purpose were known as 'trading hulks', 'accommodation hulks', or 'storage hulks'. There was no requirement to register a hulk, and the term came to include abandoned vessels of no value, or vessels that had been damaged in remote corners of the world, where repair was impractical.

In West Africa, where European traders in palm oil were not permitted to reside on land, hulks were used for living and trading quarters and as floating warehouses for the palm oil awaiting shipment to Liverpool. As the days of sail declined and steamships dominated the seas around the world, the change from sail to steam in West Africa was effectively complete by 1880.

It was no longer necessary for traders like Stuart & Douglas to own their own ships. They could trade just as effectively and more profitably by sending their cargoes of palm oil by steamship to Liverpool, using the services of agents accommodated on hulks in New Calabar, Bonny or Opobo, rather than maintain under-employed crews, who were susceptible to innumerable diseases. By 1870, there were fourteen or fifteen hulks at Bonny alone. (There is no formal record of the hulks in the rivers of the delta, as there was then no registry.) Hulks became the defining feature of the palm oil trade in the delta, and *Mimosa* became one of those features.

Worn out and useless, even as a trading vessel, *Mimosa* was dismasted, and her once-lovely Aberdeen hull, built of the centuries-old oak of Glen Tanar, was used to store the oil brought by canoe from all parts of the New Calabar river to be loaded onto steamships bound for Liverpool. Her sails and rigging were removed, and her decks were shaded with a thatch of palm leaves and raffia matting over rafters of sturdy bamboo. Holes were cut in her side, and a crane was mounted on deck to facilitate the transfer of casks from canoe to her hold and from her hold to the Liverpool-bound steamships anchored alongside. Like a small Noah's ark without Noah and the animals, she served, too, perhaps, as a house and office for Stuart & Douglas's agent and his staff until the end of each season, when the agent returned to Liverpool, leaving a clerk or two living on board until the beginning of the next.

All organic materials being subject to rapid bacterial decay in the climate of the delta, *Mimosa*'s remaining ropes would have lasted no more than two years. With her copper sheathing intact, she might have lasted for ten years; without it, she would have lasted no longer than five. After ten years, her wooden decks would have rotted, rendering her unfit even for use as a storage hulk. By that time, traders were established in offices and bungalows on shore, and hulks in the delta became a thing of the past.

Too old now, there was no further use for *Mimosa*. Abandoned and alone, she undoubtedly remained under the scorching African sun in the malaria-infested estuary, her white paint blistering, her varnish bubbling, her remaining plates of copper sheathing hanging in bedraggled ribbons, to be eventually stolen to make bracelets or necklets so that she became riddled with teredos, until she rotted in her watery graveyard on the swampy shore of the New Calabar river.

Requiescat in Pace

Mimosa's end, when it came, on a swampy creek, some six nautical miles from the sea, on the west bank of the New Calabar River, was by slow decay, until her ribs could no longer support her timbers and decks. There was none to mourn her passing, none to grieve her death.

The last entry, recorded in red ink in the *Registry of Transactions Book* in Liverpool, is to document that she was converted to a hulk in New Calabar. It is dated January 27, 1880. The final entry, written in red ink, closed her registry and the story of her life.

The final entry.

Part VIII

Passings

The romance of the tea-clippers is a thing of the past …

Andrew Shewan, *The Days of Great Sail*

Alexander Hall & Sons

Three years after *Mimosa*'s voyage to Patagonia, in 1868, James Hall died of a fatal heart attack. A fire broke out in the shipyard, threatening the *Jho Sho Maru*, a ship ready for delivery, which the Halls had built for the emperor of Japan. Fearful that this huge ship, for which he had under-estimated its contract price, would catch fire, James Hall rushed to the scene and ordered her to be pulled to the middle of the dock. The *Jho Sho Maru* was saved, and was the ship on which the Japanese navy was founded. In helping to fight the blaze, when the flames burst through the wood flooring at his feet, James Hall collapsed. He was sixty-four years of age.

Named after his grandfather, James Cochar, James Hall was, by every standard and by all opinions, a good man. Having no children of their own, he and his wife, Christina, had brought up Alexander Hall Wilson, the only surviving son of his sister, Ann. As shipyard manager, he instigated a Sick and Medical Fund, whereby, for a weekly contribution, the shipyard workers received sick pay, medical attendance and medicine and, if the worst happened, funeral expenses, and he served on the Footdee Dispensary committee, pledged to bring about better medical conditions for the poor. He also inaugurated the Saturday half day, the first shipyard manager in Britain to do so.

William Hall's child, born the year following *Mimosa*'s construction, was a daughter, who was named Christina, after his brother's wife. She died when she was four. His son, Alexander, who was fourteen when the photograph of the shipyard men was taken, became an engineer. He died in Nagasaki in 1876, aged twenty-eight, possibly of cholera or one of the many diseases that ravaged the East.

The years following Alexander's death were dark days for William Hall. His wife, Catherine, had died two years before his brother James, and a few months after James Hall's death, the shipyard went bankrupt. Ships built speculatively, like the splendid *Cairngorm*, failed to find buyers who would pay what they were worth. Others turned out to be loss-making because the contract price had been too low. A partner of a rope- and sail-making company, of which the William Hall owned 50%, absconded, and William Hall was liable for half the debt. Liabilities exceeded assets, and the banks stopped credit. By borrowing from a friend and using an advance for a ship, William Hall continued paying the wages of the shipyard workers. Finally, his back to the wall, William Hall had no alternative but to apply for sequestration and, during the three-day sale that followed, the entire shipyard stock was auctioned.

William Hall was down but not out. Helped by his surviving sons and the high standing of his family name, the firm recovered and went from strength to strength. Iron followed wood; steam replaced sail. In 1887, William Hall died aged eighty-one, and the era of clipper ships died with him. He was succeeded by his two surviving sons, William and James.

Alexander Hall & Sons, which became Alexander Hall & Co. in 1904, when the family connection ended with the younger William Hall's retirement, continued building ships of first class quality into the 20th century, making trawlers, ferries, passenger and cargo ships, minesweepers for both world wars, marine laboratories and vessels of various kinds for countries in all parts of the world, from the Sudan to Iceland. During the Second World War, a fire in the shipyard offices destroyed the old plans and all but four of the firm's hundreds of half-models. The half-model of Robert Vining's *Reindeer* is one of the four that still exists. Sadly, *Mimosa*'s has not. The shipyard lasted until 1958, when it was taken over by the neighbouring Hall Russell yard, the company William and James Hall had formed with an engineer, Thomas Russell, in order to build engines and boilers for their ships, of which their nephew, Alexander Hall Wilson, was head. Hall, Russell and Co., while it existed, gave employment to thousands of shipyard workers and hundreds of office staff, a far cry from the old shipyard staff of twenty men and two young office boys.

The grace and beauty of the clipper ship was achieved by men like William Hall, who had an intuitive instinct for beautiful, sweeping curves, and in whose blood flowed the innovative skill of James Cochar and the vision of the first Alexander Hall. With the passing of William Hall, the era of ships like *Mimosa* died with him.

Glen Tanar

Mimosa was one of the last ships to have her timber floated down the Dee. After 1853, the railway carried timber from Glen Tanar to the shipyards in Aberdeen in a more efficient, though considerably less picturesque, manner.

In the early 1890s, Glen Tanar was bought by a Manchester banker, later the Member of Parliament for East Cheshire, William Cunliffe Brooks, a descendent of an old family of Lancastrian yeomen. Entranced by the remoteness and beauty of Glen Tanar, he dedicated his wealth and energies to restoring its old roads and re-planting its forest. A church,

St Lesmo's chapel, was built by him in Glen Tanar to replace the old heather-thatched Black Chapel of the Moor that had fallen into ruin. The pews were covered with deer skin, the roof timbers were of girdled pine, and its altar was a stone taken from the Water of Tanar itself. After his death, Glen Tanar was purchased by George Coats of the Paisley thread family, who was created first Baron of Glentaner in 1916.

Two world wars have denuded Glen Tanar of much of its timber. During World War II, two units of Canadian Forestry Corps and four private contractors cut and prepared millions of cubic feet of mature trees. In 1920, a fire raged for three days and four nights and destroyed nine thousand acres of its forest; but the ancient drove roads of Fir Mounth can still be seen through the moss and weeds.

Anjer

On August 27, 1883, the volcano on the island of Krakatoa, in the Sunda Strait, erupted, sending six cubic miles of rock and lava into the sky. The sound of its explosions were heard as far away as Australia and Japan and, as a result of the volcanic dust that diffused the atmosphere the world over, brilliant sunsets were observed in Wales, England and parts of Scotland. The telegraph poles that had communicated *Mimosa*'s arrival time through the typhoon-buffeted Sunda Strait to London and Liverpool, in all her China voyages, were destroyed by *tsunami* waves as Anjer disappeared for ever beneath the sea.

Robert Vining

On January 23, 1885, five years after *Mimosa*'s last recorded entry in the *Book of Transactions*, Robert Vining died at his residence. He was seventy-seven years of age. Three broughams, carrying his two sons, various aldermen and Liverpool dignitaries, as well as William Killey, and the private carriage of the mayor of Liverpool, followed the horse-drawn hearse. The town hall flag was flown at half mast – a mark of respect normally reserved only for royalty or state or city officials; and obituaries appeared in all five Liverpool newspapers. The coffin was of oak with ornate brass mountings, and a shield was inscribed with his name, age and date of death. He was buried in the Vining family vault, in the Church of England part of Anfield Cemetery.

Paradoxically, Robert Vining is remembered today as the owner of a ship which, irrespective of her voyages to Brazil and China, gained immortality from her one voyage to Patagonia; a♦d, for some, his name has become secondary to hers and to the passengers she carried.

William Killey

Following the death of his partner, William Killey assumed total control of the company, which had been renamed William Killey & Co. since 1868, seven years before Robert Vining's death. At the time of his retirement, he owned shares in eight ships: *Barracouta*, *Bella*, *Craigmullen*, *Margaret Deane*, *Linda*, *Edward Herbert*, *Petchelee* and *David Harrison*. Having risen from the ranks of master mariner, to subscriber, to owner, he must have seen his life as the success it undoubtedly was.

Stuart & Douglas

Peter Douglas died in 1883, leaving two sons, Peter and Murray, and two daughters, Grace and Margaret. Peter Stuart died five years later, in 1888.

In the year following Peter Stuart's death, the enormous empire which he had founded with Peter Douglas was assimilated by the African Association Ltd. of Liverpool (later to become the African & Eastern Trade Corporation), and the Stuart & Douglas name disappeared.

Peter Stuart was known as a just man and an honest merchant, an accolade not given to many. A fervent believer in personal and political freedom, he saw beyond the columns of profit and loss. He paid his agents based in the West African delta well, making them more like partners than mere employees, respecting their decisions and acting upon them. His funeral was attended by that famous Liberal, William Ewart Gladstone; the mayor of Liverpool; representatives from the African Steam Company; and African Association; by one of William Killey's sons, indicating that the acquaintance between Peter Stuart and William Killey had been a long-standing one; and by his surviving sons, daughters and grandchildren. His wife Ellen predeceased him

They had nine children, who received education in Brussels and Hanover as well as in Liverpool. Their seven sons were: Hahnemann, named after the great homeopathic physician, Samuel Hahnemann; Cromwell, who died of sunstroke at Bonny, aged twenty-two; Milton, who entered the family firm; Peter, who became a Hahnemanian homeopath and, like his father, gave his services freely to those who could not afford them; Orsini; Mazzini, who established Hahnemann House in London as a museum to the founder of homeopathy; and Belmont. Their two daughters, Selina and Rachel Ann, both spoke Italian, French, German and Hebrew and, like their mother, were accomplished pianists.

George Pepperell

George Pepperell was just twenty-five when he was given charge of *Mimosa* for her voyage to Patagonia. He was clearly out of his depth in dealing with the passengers on the voyage, and his behaviour shows a lack of maturity and also a lack of seamanship.

Following his voyage to Patagonia, George Pepperell made eight subsequent voyages with *Mimosa*, all of which were to Brazil. Many of his crewmen were from the criminal class and behaved accordingly. When they were drunk and disorderly, violent or abusive, as frequently they were, he disciplined them with a firm hand, but was always, somewhat naively, prepared to believe the best of them, instead of the worst.

When *Mimosa* was sold to Stuart & Douglas, after his last voyage with her, he captained ten more ships, continuing on the South American run to Brazil, and ending his career with the Brazilian and River Plate Steam Navigation Co., in 1878, when he was fifty.

Of all *Mimosa*'s five masters he was the longest serving, captaining her for six years, and through eleven voyages, which clearly demonstrates the trust William Killey had in him. Perhaps, too, he was the one who loved her most, who took the most pride in her performance and her appearance. She was the ship on which he grew in confidence and experience, enabling him to pass from sail to the modern age of steel and steam.

The Painting and Figurehead

The painting of *Mimosa* has disappeared, along with the names of whoever commissioned and painted it. Having been acquired by the Parker Galley in London, a gallery specializing in maritime art, it was bought in 1978 by a collector living in the Isle of Wight. Upon his death, the painting again changed hands, when the collection was sold, and to date has not been traced. Somewhere, the painted likeness of *Mimosa* exists. Her original figurehead – her guiding spirit – has also disappeared. What happened to it after it was removed, a few days prior to her voyage to Patagonia, is not known. Perhaps it was sold for a few shillings to a retired master mariner, who desired a memento of his sailing days to grace the outside of his cottage. Perhaps, it is exhibited in a museum of maritime art, or has been nailed over the doorway of an inn or public house in some seaport town where, one hopes, her painted blue eyes look out to sea.

The Halton Castle

The *Halton Castle* arrived back in Liverpool from Iquitos, on the Amazon basin on the northwest coast of South America, on May 4, 1865. It sailed for Valparaiso on June 10, almost two weeks after *Mimosa* sailed for Patagonia. It made subsequent voyages to the West Indies and South America, and was eventually sold to Angel Brothers and sailed into total obscurity. The *Halton Castle* is remembered only as the ship which, through delay in returning to Liverpool, was unable to transport a desperate group of passengers to an unknown part of the world, and the fame that might have been its belongs to another.

Michael Daniel Jones

In 1882, seventeen years after *Mimosa's* voyage to New Bay, Michael D Jones visited Patagonia to see for himself the towns of Puerto Madryn, Rawson, Dolavon, Gaiman and Trelew. His sons, when they grew up, left Wales for Argentina, where Mihangel became a doctor at the British Hospital in Buenos Aires, practising first in the towns of Suipacha and Junín, in the same province. Llwyd followed his father's dream. After training as a civil engineer in London and Germany, he went to Patagonia, where he became a staunch supporter of the ideals of the colony, and married the daughter of Lewis Jones. He was murdered in the store of the Chubut Trading Company, of which he was manager, by the Parker gang, whose leaders were nicknamed Butch Cassidy and the Sundance Kid.

Michael Daniel Jones died in 1898, when he was seventy-six, crippled by grief at Llwyd's brutal death. The ongoing expenses of keeping his dream of *Y Wladfa* a reality forced him to sell Bodiwan, his home and seat of the Independent College that his father had founded. He was worn out by defending *Y Wladfa* against detractors, who exaggerated or lied about the conditions, or who claimed, like one of the British consuls in Buenos Aires, that the failure of the settlement in the first year was due to the laziness of the colonists during the weeks after landing. He is buried in the Old Chapel burial ground at Llanuwchllyn. Anne Lloyd Jones lived to be ninety-three and died in Wales.

Love Jones Parry

In 1868, Love Jones Parry won the Caernarfon seat for the Liberals, but lost it in the next election. He won the Caernarfon Boroughs seat in 1882, which he held until 1886, and was made a baronet by Gladstone, for his services to the Liberal Party.

In 1891, Thomas Love Duncombe Jones Parry died. The estate was sold and half a ton of gold dishes was packed in carts and transported by train for auction in London, to pay for his considerable debts. He is buried at the family church of St Pedrog's in Madryn. Of Madryn Castle itself nothing today remains, except for the ruins of a gatehouse, and the land has been converted to a caravan park.

Puerto Madryn is, by contrast, one of the fastest growing cities in Patagonia, with vigorous industries in tourism, commercial fishing and aluminium mining. The Valdéz Peninsula is a designated UNESCO World Heritage Site, and, in 1999, Puerto Madryn was twinned with Nefyn, the closest village to Madryn Castle.

Robert Nagle

Robert Nagle was the last-moment replacement as passenger steward on the voyage out to Patagonia. He was responsible for cleaning the passengers' accommodation area and arranging meal shifts. After landing, he was put in charge of the colony's small sailing boats, among which was the secondhand longboat, purchased in Liverpool and used mainly to transport food and stores from Carmen de Patagones or Buenos Aires to the colony. The longboat, intended to carry food from New Bay to the Chuput, was irreparably damaged a few days after arrival, when trying to navigate the dangerous bar across the mouth of the river.

He made frequent voyages to Buenos Aires and Carmen de Patagones, on a schooner given to the colony by the Argentine government: the ill-fated *Denby*, which was eventually condemned as unseaworthy by a port official in Buenos Aires.

In January 1868, Robert Nagle sailed the *Denby* to Patagones, accompanied by five of the strongest young men, in order to collect supplies for the colony, then in desperate straits and on the brink of dispersal to other areas in the provinces of Santa Fe and Rio Negro. Patagones was reached safely, and the little schooner was loaded with food and two working oxen. It left Patagones on February 16, 1868, and was never seen again. In a precarious state of repair to begin with, the oxen on board evidently damaged her more. Either a leak was sprung by a hoof, or the load was shifted to one side by the animals roaming round, causing it to capsize or fill up with water.

On board with Nagle, and presumed drowned, were James Jones, Thomas Pennant Evans (Twmi Dimol), David Davies, David Jones and his brother George, who had all been in their teens or early twenties when they had boarded *Mimosa* in Liverpool. Neither the *Denby* nor the bodies of the men were ever recovered.

Richard Jones Berwyn

Richard Berwyn, *Mimosa*'s only passenger purser, recorded the colony's births, marriages and deaths for ten years, from the date of sailing from Liverpool in 1865. Although the original register was lost in the disastrous flood that occurred in the Chubut valley in 1899, copies of its entries were sent to and maintained in Wales, and remain a valuable genealogical source of the early settlers in the colony. A man of intelligence and intellect, he held official positions as secretary to the Welsh courts and governing council, and was the first post master. When the colony came under Argentine jurisdiction, he was elected private secretary to the first governor, Dr Luis Fontana. Under less far-sighted governors, he was imprisoned for his stand in maintaining the rights of the Welsh. He published the first Welsh newspaper, *Y Brut*, and wrote the first Welsh text book for the colony's schools. He married Elizabeth Pritchard, the young widow of Thomas Pennant Evans (Twmi Dimol), one of the men who drowned when the *Denby* sank. Richard Berwyn died on Christmas Day in 1917, and, to this day, he is held in great respect.

Thomas Greene

On November 10, 1865, when the colony appeared to be on the brink of collapse, Thomas Greene left Patagonia on a small schooner called *Mary Helen*, along with others that included Lewis Jones, Lewis Jones's wife and brother, Stephen.

On reaching Buenos Aires, Thomas Greene wrote to his brothers, relating some of his experiences in Patagonia and explaining his decision to leave. As he conveyed to H G: initially, he had fully intended to remain, and 'nothing but want', resulting from chronic lack of food, the uncertainty of receiving further supplies from the Argentine government, and the Emigration Committee's inability to honour the terms of his contract made him decide to leave with Lewis Jones. Another reason for his decision to leave was loneliness: he was lonely for his brothers and felt increasingly isolated, since he was not Welsh.

After a short spell in a boarding house in Buenos Aires, he struck south again. He went to the wild, coastal part of the south of the province of Buenos Aires, called the Tuyú, and worked as the first doctor in the area, where his survival skills, acquired in Patagonia, stood him in good stead. He lived in a primitive adobe dwelling thatched with bulrushes, where the cooking was done over an open fire in the middle of the floor, and his bed was a blanket on the bare floor. In the epidemic of cholera that struck Tuyú in 1866, he frequently buried the dead with his own hands, when their relatives, in terror of the epidemic, refused to do so.

When he was twenty-five, he went to Uruguay, where he became a physician in a small town called San José, which consisted of an unpaved plaza and a few dirt streets. Ultimately, he became physician at the British Hospital in Montevideo, when the hospital was located in old port, the exact location of which is now unknown. On a return visit to Ireland, he met and married a young Englishwoman, whose brother, a clergyman in Ireland, was the future father of the poet laureate, Cecil Day Lewis.

For Thomas Greene, too, *Mimosa* was a turning point in his life, for he remained in South America for the remainder of his professional life, maintaining a contact of sorts with the family of Michael D Jones, through Michael D Jones's son, Mihangel. He was *Mimosa*'s only doctor. He died in Ireland in January 1922.

Y Wladfa

The first years of Y *Wladfa* were difficult beyond imagining. Difficulties appeared insurmountable. Again and again it came perilously to the brink of collapse. Again and again, with help from Guillermo Rawson and under the influence of Lewis Jones' fierce persuasion, they started all over again. After two years, the population of Y *Wladfa* had been reduced to ninety, most of whom were women and children.

Against all odds and despite incredible sufferings and hardships, the colony in Patagonia survived. Every day that passed was a triumph. Every day without mishap was a miracle that gave *Mimosa*'s people hope to carry on. Courage, they already possessed in abundance. In time, *mintai Mimosa*, as *Mimosa's* people are known in Wales and Patagonia, adapted to their new land. The children, better fed, adequately clothed and robust, began to thrive. The weakest and sickest having died in the first few months, some from diseases they had contracted in Wales or Liverpool, the children born and raised in Patagonia were strong and healthy. Thirty years passed before the colony had another doctor, after Thomas Greene left at the end of 1865.

The Tehuelche Indians, whom they so feared, eventually came. On April 19, 1866, at the double wedding of Edwin Cynrig Roberts and Ann Jones, and Ann's brother, Richard, to Hannah Davies, some five months after *Mimosa* sailed from New Bay, an old *cacique* and his wife appeared. Neither could speak the other's language, but a bond of mutual trust was formed – a bond that was unique in any previous contact between European and indigenous peoples – as a woman gave the *cacique's* wife her baby to hold. In time, the Tehuelche taught the Welsh to ride the horses they gave them, and traded guanaco skins, which kept them warmer than their Welsh-spun blankets, in exchange for butter and *bara* – a word which from henceforth became the Tehuelches' word for bread.

With the increase in numbers from other places, some of *Mimosa*'s people pushed further west along the valley, to the foothills of the Andes, and established farms in the most beautiful and verdant areas of South America. Some went to more settled areas in the province of Santa Fe. A few returned to Wales. A few, like Joseph Seth Jones, relocated for a time in the Falkland Islands. Some went to Saskatchewan, in Canada. Most remained in Patagonia, founding towns like Gaiman, Dolavon, Treorky, Esquel and Trevelin, and became an inspiration to others in Wales and beyond.

The Final Word

A new prosperity has come to Aberdeen. Today, massive oil rigs and tankers take the black gold from the North Sea where once Footdee men fished with mussel-baited lines for a different kind of harvest. The open space where generations of fishermen dried their nets is now a golf links, and the sheds and outhouses where once their wives and daughters gutted fish or baited lines of mussels have long gone. In their place are car parks and a children's adventure playground, and the old slate-roofed fisher houses of Footdee fetch the sort of prices that only highly-paid professionals can afford.

Liverpool is now a city where the houses of the merchant princes have been converted into flats, offices and centres of learning. The mansion which Peter Stuart built in Seaforth, with its marbled interiors and Italianate gardens, its library, music room and its art gallery of priceless masters, was demolished in the 1920s, and a council housing estate now stands on its site. The Clarence Graving Dock has long been closed. The Victoria Dock has gone, and the few docks that remain resemble derelict gigantic swimming pools, their empty vastness a sad and ghostly reminder of the commercial wealth that once was Liverpool.

A few ships and passenger liners, carrying emigrants to less desolate parts of the New World than Patagonia, still dock at Liverpool, whose skyline is still, for many, their last view of England; and ferries and Sea Cats make the twice-daily trips to Dublin, Belfast or the Isle of Man, with cars and tourist buses in their holds.

Mimosa was one of the last clippers to be built with the Aberdeen bow. In 1854, the year after her construction, the Tonnage laws changed, no longer necessitating the bow which had revolutionized shipping by creating unsurpassed speed in merchant sailing ships. *Mimosa* was part of the maritime history of the swiftest and most beautiful ships the world had ever seen, which rose, flourished and passed for ever within the span of an average human lifetime. The speed of the clipper ships was never equalled by any sailing vessel, before or since. They became myths in their own lifetimes, and the myth surrounding *Mimosa* was not based on fast voyages or legendary races. She sailed on all oceans, to every corner of the world – to China, the Malaysian and Indonesian archipelagos, Patagonia, Brazil and West Africa. She knew monsoons, storms and millpond calms. She was an aristocrat of her class, with fine lines that were built for speed, a true princess of the seas.

By the end of the 1860s, clippers were no longer being built entirely of wood, but were a composite of iron and wood. When the Suez Canal opened, steamers made the journey from England to China and the East in a third of the time that clippers had done, and in the fierce scramble for cargoes, the clippers were soon squeezed out. Only large cargoes paid profits, and the clippers, for all their speed, were never designed to carry large cargoes. For a while, there was some business in transporting coal and manufactured goods to the west coast of South America and returning with hides, nitrates and guano. In 1914, when the Panama Canal opened, that trade, too, was killed. With no hopes of new cargoes, ship owners abandoned their once-lovely clippers in their last ports of call, stripped them of everything that could be sold, converted them into hulks or left them to rot. Men like Robert Vining and William Killey, with their little pretensions and limitless visions, their syndicates of merchants, retired master mariners and gentlemen, widows, with or without means, chandlers, plumbers and drapers; or merchant traders like Peter Stuart and Peter Douglas, with their own fleets of ships, which they sent to the far reaches of the known world, with their high philosophical ideals and wide-ranging passions that were unrelated to their businesses, disappeared, and hard-headed, economy-driven men like Alfred Holt and

Samuel Cunard changed the culture of ship owning for ever.

Mimosa was part of four of the most important commercial trades of the 19th century: the tea trade, the sugar trade, the cotton and the palm oil trade. She knew the most beautiful places, and the most desolate. She made twenty-seven voyages across the oceans of the world – surely a record among clippers – and three runs between one home port and another.

Mimosa was part, too, of a venture to a little-known part of the world which, against all odds and despite incredible sufferings and hardships, survived and prospered. Despite drought, flood and the scarcity of food, despite the harshness of the climate, despite death and the ache of *hiraeth* (homesickness) *Mimosa*'s people persevered in their new land, and, in time, others joined them, from a settlement in Brazil, from the Welsh communities in the United States, and from Wales itself. In the midst of grief and despair there was hope, moments of joy in the birth of a child, the comfort of the touch of a toil-roughened hand on a tear-wet cheek. The flame of whatever impelled *Mimosa*'s people to go to Patagonia never died. It sometimes flickered dangerously low; but it was never extinguished.

Twenty-seven people, mostly unknown except for their names, at one time or another had held shares in the little clipper. Some would never have seen her, and it is doubtful that most had any interest in her, except as a means of furthering their commercial interests, enhancing their prestige, defraying their debts, or augmenting their incomes. She had six masters, on whose navigational skills her survival depended and her performance was judged. More than four hundred men enlisted on her as crews, of whom twenty-eight deserted and an unknown number were shanghaied or crimped. Twenty-four apprentices gained their knowledge of seamanship on her. Eleven, among whom were five Welsh children, were known to have lost their lives on her. Others, for whom their last sight before sinking beneath the waves was the wash of her stern, fell overboard.

To the Welsh passengers who sailed in her, whose children died or were born on her, who were married on her, who wept, laughed, prayed or kept their thoughts silent on her, she represented a temporary abode, which took them from the familiar past to an unknown future. Many of those who met on the voyage to Patagonia, later married there. Young, unmarried men found wives among the families with daughters, some of whom had known one another in Wales. The older men, who had been left widowed with children, found younger wives, with whom they had second families. The women travelling alone, or as servants, found husbands, as did the young wives who were suddenly widowed when their husbands died or were drowned.

The day of disembarkation at New Bay, on the desolate beach that is now called Puerto Madryn, is celebrated every twenty-eighth day of July, throughout Wales and Patagonia. The day, known as *Gŵyl y Glaniad* (the Celebration of the Landing) is a public holiday throughout the province of Chubut and an especial day of celebration and thanksgiving for the Welsh in Patagonia.

In every history, book, and all the correspondence that have been written, and are still being written about *Y Wladfa*, *Mimosa*'s name is mentioned. She is lauded in poetry and song; and in 1965, a special *Mimosa* stamp was issued in Argentina to commemorate the centenary of the founding of the province of Chubut. *Mimosa* was part of a movement that went far beyond the voyage itself, and she became a symbol for the courage it took to endure the hardships, tragedies and uncertainties encountered in the desolation that was Patagonia.

Fate, chance, destiny, or whatever it be called, has given *Mimosa* a place in history, irrespective of her cargo-carrying voyages.

The ripples cast by her cutwater which spread from Liverpool to Patagonia as she sailed into immortality have not abated. Her name lives on, inseparable from the names of her people – the only passengers she is known to have carried.

Appendix I

Mimosa's Masters, Voyages and 'Runs'

Thomas Kemp

1. Aberdeen – Newcastle (in ballast)
   July 5, 1853 – July 19, 1853
   (National Archives, Kew, BT 98/3423)

2. North Shield – Rio de Janeiro
   July 28, 1853 – March 11, 1854
   (National Archives, BT 98/3423)

3. Liverpool – Shanghai
   June 8, 1854 – May 10, 1855
   (National Archives, BT 98/4205)

4. Liverpool – Shanghai
   June 5, 1855 – January 14, 1856
   (National Archives, BT 98/4546)

5. Liverpool – Shanghai
   February 19, 1856 – January 18, 1857
   (National Archives, BT 98/4788)

6. Run from London – Liverpool
   February 10, 1857 – February 17, 1857
   (National Archives, BT 98/4788)

7. Liverpool – Rio de Janeiro
   March 19, 1857 – October 10, 1857
   (National Archives, BT 98/4788)

Trevanion Hugo

8. Liverpool – Rio de Janeiro
   November 17, 1857 – May 23, 1858
   (National Archives BT 98/5122)

9. Liverpool – Rio de Janeiro
   July 2, 1858 – November 23, 1858
   (National Archives, BT 98/5122)

10. Liverpool – Rio de Janeiro
    February 3, 1859 – August 1, 1859
    (National Archives, BT 98/5591)

11. Liverpool – Rio de Janeiro
    October 26, 1859 – April 25, 1860
    (National Archives, BT 98/6283)

12. Liverpool – Rio de Janeiro and Mauritius
    June 16, 1860 – January 28, 1861
    (National Maritime Museum, Greenwich, BE 1529/1/2/3/62)

13. Run from Bristol – Liverpool

February 11, 1861 – February 23, 1861

(National Maritime Museum, BE 1529/1/2/3/62)

14. Liverpool – Mauritius

March 31, 1861 – October 15, 1861

(National Maritime Museum, BE 1529/1/2/3/62)

15. Liverpool – Rio de Janeiro

December 2, 1861 – May 10, 1862

(National Maritime Museum, BE 1529/2/2/2/35)

Archibald Johnson

16. Liverpool – Bahia

July 14, 1862 – February 2, 1863

(National Archives, BT 99/140)

17. Liverpool – Foochow

March 27, 1863 – March 2, 1864

(Maritime History Archives, Newfoundland)

George Pepperell

18. London – Rio de Janeiro

April 21, 1864 – December 6, 1864

(Maritime History Archives, Newfoundland)

19. Liverpool – Pernambuco
    December 17, 1864 – April 5, 1865.
    (National Archives, BT 99/230)

20. Liverpool – Nueva Bay, Patagonia
    May 28, 1865 – November 25, 1865
    (National Archives, BT 99/230 XP 918)

21. Liverpool – Bahia
    December 13, 1865 – May 5, 1866
    (Maritime History Archives, Newfoundland)

22. Liverpool – Bahia
    June 12, 1866 – December 27, 1866
    (Maritime History Archives, Newfoundland)

23. Liverpool – Pernambuco
    February 23, 1867 – August 21, 1867
    (Maritime History Archives, Newfoundland)

24. Liverpool – Bahia
    October 18, 1867 – April 8, 1868
    (Maritime History Archives, Newfoundland)

25. Liverpool – the Brazils
    June 3, 1868 – November 19, 1868
    (Maritime History Archives, Newfoundland)

26. Liverpool – Bahia

January 5, 1869 – July 16, 1869

(Maritime History Archives, Newfoundland)

27. Liverpool – Bahia

September 23, 1869 – April 9, 1870

(Liverpool Record Office, Liverpool)

28. Liverpool – Pernambuco

May 20, 1870 – November 4, 1870

(Liverpool Record Office, Liverpool)

Stephen Goodman/John Campbell

29. Liverpool – New Calabar

March 16, 1871 – March 11, 1872

(Maritime History Archives, Newfoundland)

John Campbell

30. Liverpool – New Calabar

May 11, 1872 – October, 1872

(Maritime History Archives, Newfoundland)

Appendix 2

Mimosa's People –
the Passengers on the Voyage to Patagonia and their ages[44]

Mountain Ash:

John JONES (61)
Elizabeth JONES (53)
Ann JONES (18)
Margaret JONES (15)
Richard JONES (20)
John JONES (28)
Mary (MORGAN) JONES (27)
Thomas Harries JONES (16)

Daniel EVANS (30)
Mary (JONES) EVANS (26)
Elizabeth EVANS (5))
John Daniel EVANS (3)
William AWSTIN (14)
Thomas Tegai AWSTIN (11)

John E. DAVIES (26)
Cecilia DAVIES (24)

Aaron JENKINS (34)
Rachel (EVANS) JENKINS (32)
James JENKINS (2)
Richard JENKINS (1)

James JONES (27)
Sarah JONES (24)
Mary Anne JONES (2)
James JONES (baby)

Mary JONES (22)

Mary LEWIS

Thomas JENKINS (23)
William JENKINS (18)

Elizabeth JONES

John DAVIES (18)

Thomas WILLIAMS (60)
Mary WILLIAMS (55)

William RICHARDS (19)

David JOHN (31)

Thomas HARRIS (31)
Sarah HARRIS (31)
William HARRIS (11)
John HARRIS (9)
Thomas HARRIS (5)
Daniel HARRIS (baby)
Thomas THOMAS (26)

Aberdare:

Reverend Abraham MATTHEWS (32)
Gwenllian MATTHEWS (23)
Mary Anne MATTHEWS (8 months)

235

Thomas DAVIES (40)
Elizabeth (JONES) DAVIES (42)
David DAVIES (18)
Hannah DAVIES (16)
Elizabeth DAVIES (12)
Ann DAVIES (7)
Evan JONES (19)
Thomas JONES (15)
David JONES (12)
Elizabeth JONES (10)

Evan DAVIES (25)
Ann DAVIES (30)
Margaret Ann DAVIES (baby)

Mary Ann JOHN (24)

Joshua JONES (22)

Brynmawr:
James DAVIES (18)

Bridgend:
John Murray THOMAS (19)

Anglesey:
William HUGHES (32)
Jane HUGHES
Jane HUGHES (infant)

Elizabeth PRITCHARD (19)

Bangor:
Robert THOMAS (29)
Mary THOMAS (30)
Mary THOMAS (5)
Catherine Jane THOMAS (2)

Eleanor WILLIAMS (24)
Elizabeth WILLIAMS (infant)

Elizabeth ROBERTS (19)

Bethesda:
Grace ROBERTS (25)

Anne JONES (23)

Llanfairfechan:
Baptist Minister Robert Meirion
    WILLIAMS (51)
Richard Howell WILLIAMS (18)

Caernarfon:
Richard HUGHES (18)

Stephen JONES (19)

Bala:
William R. JONES (31)
Catherine JONES (31)
Mary JONES (2)
Jane JONES (16 months)

236

Ganllwyd:

Maurice HUMPHREYS (27)

Elizabeth Harriet HUMPHREYS (21)

Reverend Lewis HUMPHREYS (27)

John HUMPHREYS (22)

Llandrillo:

Robert DAVIES (45)

Catherine DAVIES (36)

William DAVIES (7)

Henry DAVIES (5)

John DAVIES (11 months)

Ffestiniog:

Griffith PRICE (27)

James Benjamin REES (23)

Griffith SOLOMON (23)

Elizabeth SOLOMON (30)

Elizabeth SOLOMON (13 months)

John Moelwyn ROBERTS (20)

John ROBERTS (27)

Mary ROBERTS (27)

Thomas ROBERTS (2)

Mary ROBERTS (infant)

John ROBERTS (infant)

Denbigh:

Joseph Seth JONES (20)

Rhosllanerchrugog:

John HUGHES (30)

Elizabeth HUGHES (39)

William John HUGHES (10)

Myfanwy Mary HUGHES (4)

John Samuel HUGHES (2)

Henry HUGHES (baby)

Griffith HUGHES (36)

Mary HUGHES (35)

Jane HUGHES (11)

Griffith Edward HUGHES (9)

David HUGHES (6)

Llanfechan:

John ELLIS (38)

Thomas ELLIS (36)

Richard ELLIS (27)

Frances ELLIS (27)

Aberystwyth:

Lewis DAVIES (24)

Rachel DAVIES (28)

Thomas DAVIES (1 month)

David WILLIAMS (21)

John MORGANS (29)

Liverpool:

George JONES (16)

David JONES (15)

Hugh HUGHES (Cadvan) (40)

Elizabeth HUGHES (45)

Jane HUGHES (20)

David HUGHES (6)

Llewelyn HUGHES (4)

Jane WILLIAMS (24)

Edward PRICE (41)

Martha Ellen PRICE (38)

Edward PRICE (16)

Ellen PRICE (2)

William DAVIES (36)

Ann OWEN

Birkenhead:

John WILLIAMS (30)

Elizabeth WILLIAMS (31)

John WILLIAMS (4)

Elizabeth WILLIAMS (2)

Watkin William Pritchard WILLIAMS (30)

Watkin Wesley WILLIAMS (27)

Elizabeth Louisa WILLIAMS (28)

William WILLIAMS (21)

Catherine WILLIAMS

Catherine HUGHES (24)

Seecombe:

William ROBERTS (27)

Manchester:

Rhydderch HUWS (33)

Sarah HUWS (37)

Jane HUWS (17)

Rhydderch Meurig HUWS (4)

Thomas Pennant EVANS (29)

Abergynolwyn:

William HUGHES (33)

Anne LEWIS (35)

Mary HUGHES (infant)

Tregethin:

William Thomas RHYS (25)

Notes

1. Information on Alexander Hall's life and ancestry was obtained from 'The World's First Clipper', by Boyd cable, *Mariner's Mirror, Vol. 29, No. 2, April 1943*.

2. Alexander Hall & Co. Builder's List, City of Aberdeen Art Gallery and Museum Collections.

3. *Aberdeen Journal,* June 22, 1853.

4. Document No. BT 98/3423, Public Records Office, Kew, Surrey.

5. From north to south, the names of the docks were: Huskisson, Sandon, Wellington, Bramley Moore, Nelson, Stanley, Collingwood, Salisbury, Clarence, Trafalgar, Victoria, Waterloo, Prince's, George's, Canning, Salthouse, Albert, Duke's, Wapping, King's, Queen's, Brunswick, Toxteth. Fourteen more were built after 1853, namely, the Hornby, Alexandra, Langton, Brocklebank, Canada, Kedling Cove Half Tide, Mining, West Side, Union and Cobourg, Brunswick, Half Tide, Toxteth, Harrington, Herculaneum and Gladstone Docks.

6. *Customs and Excise Register* No. C/EX/4/4 Vol. 73, No. 314, Merseyside Museum, Liverpool.

7. *Captains' Registers of Lloyd's of London*, MS 18567/9, Guildhall Library, London.

8. A letter written by William Killey in March 1884, held in the Liverpool Public Library, to an undisclosed shareholder in the barque *Bella,* 'Dear Sir, Enclosed please find statement of account of the 13th voyage of the *Bella* together with cheque, being the balance of your 12/64th shares of the dividend, receipt of which kindly acknowledge. In view of the depression of freights in all quarters of the globe we trust you will now consider the result of this voyage satisfactory. The *Bella* is now loading here a cargo of coal for Valparaiso and a port, and will sail during the course of the present week. We remain, Dear Sir ...'

9 According to *Gore's Liverpool Directory*, in 1853 the office of Robert Vining, Shipbroker, was located in 16 Chapel Street, William Killey's in 19 Moss Street. By 1880, they had a common office in 18 Chapel Street.

10 The transactions are documented in *Registry of Transactions Book*, Vol. 1, p. 116, Vol. III, P. 393, and Vol. IV, P. 512, Merseyside Maritime Museum, Liverpool.

11 *Captains' Registers of Lloyd's of London*, MS 18567/1-87, Guildhall.

12 A supercargo, from the Spanish *sobre cargo*, was one who was over or in charge of cargo. Often a relative of the owner, he handled the commercial side of the ship's trade affairs when in port – selling the merchandise at the ports to which the vessel was sailing, buying cargo for shipment homeward. He had authority to change a ship's course and direct it to ports where cargo might be loaded, his authority superseding the master's.

13 *Halifax Acadian Recorder*, p. 1, col. 6, April 12, 1856.

14 Will of John Lloyd, SA 1837/19, National Library of Wales, NLW 5442C.

15 National Library of Wales, NLW 5442C.

16 *Yr Herald Cymraeg*, March 17, 1866 (Translation supplied by Elvey MacDonald).

17 In *Lloyd's Captains' Registers*, MS 18J67/11, in the Guildhall Library in London, there are no fewer than eleven Pepperells listed, and George Pepperell frequently signed his name as 'George Pepperell Junior' in *Mimosa's* logs.

18 Bangor Manuscripts 11456.

19 Whatever the intentions of both parties, both ended by breaking the terms of the contract. 'Board and Lodging' at New Bay did not exist and Thomas Greene died not receive any remuneration, let alone the agreed salary of £100. He departed from the colony at the beginning of November 1865, with Lewis Jones and others, on the *Mary Helen*.

According to a letter published in the *Liverpool Mercury* two months later, 'It was nothing but actual want that compelled him to this step. He considered that the agreement between the committee and himself was broken in consequence, and it was with great reluctance that he did so, as he had fully made up his mind to stay amongst them.'

20 *Customs and Excise Register*, Vol. 73, The Maritime Museum, Liverpool.

21 Bangor Manuscripts 11456.

22 Bangor Manuscripts 11456.

23 Bangor Manuscripts 11456.

24 *Baner ac Amserau Cymru*, 19 August 1863.

25 This ticket is in the possession of Oscar E Jones of Trelew, an ancestor of Abraham Matthews, to whom it was issued.

26 From the prospectus distributed by the Welsh Emigration Society, quoted in *Correspondence Respecting the Establishment of a Welsh Colony on the River Chaput, in Patagonia*, London, 1867, p. 27, National Archives, Kew.

27 Francis Mitchell, Matthew Burgess and Lars Petersen. *Agreement and Account of Crew*, BT99/230. National Archives.

28 Ships loaded their cargo in dock, but were towed out and anchored in the river, to receive their passengers, who were ferried out by steam- or row-boats from the landing stage at Pier Head, after the crew had boarded.

29 Bangor Manuscripts 11456.

30 This information was conveyed in a letter from Dr John Greene to his relatives in Ireland, which is in the private papers of Dr John Greene's youngest daughter, Sra Carmen Greene de Lombardini of Vedia, Province of Buenos Aires, who gave the author access to it, before her death in 1998.

31 According to Liverpool port historian, Michael J Stammers, there were

two pilot stations, one at the Bar, seven miles out from Liverpool, and one off Anglesey. A Pilot schooner would be stationed at each, to collect and deliver pilots from and to outward and inward bound ships.

[32] National Library of Wales, MS 18176B.

[33] University of Bangor Rare Books Department, BMS 78627.

[34] Translated from the Welsh by Elvey MacDonald, the great-great grandson of Edwin Cynrig Roberts.

[35] Some years later, his bones were found, identified by some scraps of paper from a notebook he had had. They were found a few miles away from the valley he was so eager to find; he was either on his way back to the beach, having found it, or had died of thirst before he reached the river.

[36] Abraham Matthews, *Hanes yr Wladfa Gymraeg ym Mhatagonia*.

[37] 'The Welsh Colony in Patagonia' a letter to the *Liverpool Mercury*, BMS 78627 (AX15 GWL).

[38] In *Y Faner*, April 5, 1865, Michael D Jones stipulated that 'the ship will stay in the Bay for a month, if necessary, to allow everybody enough time to carry their possessions to their final destination.' (Translated by Elvey MacDonald) The ship then expected to sail was, of course, the *Halton Castle*.

[39] Document No. BT99/230, The National Archives, Kew.

[40] Maritime History Archives, Memorial University, Newfoundland.

[41] *Lloyd's List*, March 23, 1871.

[42] *Lloyd's List*, March 27, 1871.

[43] One reason why *Mimosa* was not registered in *Lloyd's Register* before 1875 is that, until then, the Liverpool Registry was entirely separate from *Lloyd's*.

[44] I have listed some passengers with their families, with whom they were undoubtedly travelling, and not from the towns where they were living or working.

Bibliography, Sources
and Background Reading

The history of the clipper ship in general

Cable, Boyd, "The World's First Clipper", *The Mariner's Mirror*, Vol. 29, No. 2, April 1943.

Campbell, George, *China Tea Clippers*, Adlard Coles, London, 1974.

Kemp, Peter, *The History of Ships*, Grange Books, 2002.

MacGregor, David R, *Fast Sailing Ships: Their Design and Construction, 1775-1875*, Nautical Publishing Co. Ltd., 1973.

MacGregor, David R, *The Tea Clippers: Their History and Development 1833-1875*, (2nd Edition), Naval Institute Press, Annapolis, Md.

Shewan, Andrew, *Great Days of Sail*, Porcupine Press, 1996.

Whipple, A B C, *The Clipper Ships*, Time Life Books, 1980.

Alexander Hall & Sons, Footdee and Glen Tanar

Allardyce, Ann D B ("A Lady, a Native of Aberdeen"), *Footdee in the Last Century*, A. Brown & Co., Aberdeen, 1872.

Buchan Watt, V J, *The Book of Banchory*, Oliver & Boyd, Edinburgh, 1947.

Hamilton, Henry, *The County of Aberdeen,* Collins, Glasgow, 1960.

MacDonald. A, and Philip, J.B., (Editors), *The Deeside Field*, The Rosemount Press, Aberdeen, 1925.

Morgan, Diane, *Footdee and her Shipyards*, Denburn Books, Aberdeen, 1997.

Taylor, Brian, "A Way of Life, The Story of Footdee", *Leopard Magazine*, Aberdeen, September and October, 1976.

Alexander Hall & Co. Builder's List, City of Aberdeen & Museum Collections.

Ship Construction in the 19th Century

Clark, Arthur H, *The Clipper Ship Era*, 7 C's Press Inc., 1970.

Davies, Ralph, *The Rise of the English Shipping Industry in the 17th and 18th Centuries*, Macmillan, 1962.

Frazer, J G, *The Golden Bough*, Macmillan & Co., 1923. (Abridged edition.)

Jarvis, Rupert C, "Fractional Shareholding in British Merchant Shipping with Special Reference to the 64ths", *The Mariner's Mirror*, Vol. 45, 1959.

Lundy, Derek, *The Way of a Ship*, Knopf, Canada, 2002.

MacGregor, David R, "Tendering and Contract Procedure in Merchant Shipyards in the Middle of the Nineteenth Century", *The Mariner's Mirror*, Vol. 48, November 1962.

Moll, F, "The History of Wood-Preserving in Shipping", *The Mariner's Mirror*, Vol. 12, 1926.

The port of Liverpool and its history

Baines, Thomas, *History of the Commerce and Town of Liverpool and of the Rise of Manufacturing Industry in the Adjoining Counties*, Liverpool: Published by the Author. London: Longman, Brown, Green and Longmans, 1852.

Michael K Stammers, *The Passage Makers*, Teredo Books Ltd., 1978.

Bibliography, Sources and Background reading

The China Tea Trade

Campbell, George, *op. cit.*

Encyclopaedia Britannica, Eleventh Edition, Vol. XXVI.

Goodwin, Jason, *A Time for Tea*, Knopf, 1991.

MacGregor, David R, *The Tea Clippers: Their History and Development 1833-1875* (with special reference to *Mimosa*'s voyages from China to London).

Wild, Antony, *The East India Company Book of Tea*, Harper Collins, London, 1994.

Wales in the 19th Century, Patagonia, Y Wladfa

Bauer, John, "The Welsh in Patagonia: An Example of Nationalistic Migration", *The Hispanic American Historical Review*, Duke University Press, Vol. XXXIV, No. 4, November 1954.

Davies, John, *A History of Wales*, Penguin Books, 1994.

Jones, Lewis, *La colonia galesa*, Editorial El Regional, Rawson, Chubut. (Originally published as *Y Wladfa Gymreig*, Caernarfon, 1898.)

Jones, Thomas (Glan Camwy), *Historia de los comienzos de la colonia en la Patagonia*, Biblioteca Popular, Agustín Alvarez, Trelew, Chubut, translated into Spanish by Fernando Coronato. (Originally published as *Hanes Cychwyniad y Wladfa yn Mhatagonia.*)

MacDonald, Elvey, *Yr Hirdaith*, Gomer, 1999.

Matthews, Abraham, *Crónica de la Colonia Galesa*, Editorial Raigal, Buenos Aires, 1954, translated into Spanish by Frances Evelyn Roberts. (Originally published as *Hanes y Wladfa Gymreig yn Mhatagonia*, Aberdare, 1894.)

Williams, Glyn, *The Desert and the Dream*, University of Wales Press, 1975.

Documents pertaining to the voyage to Patagonia

The Diary of Joseph Seth Jones, National Library of Wales Manuscript 18176B, published as *Dyddiadur Mimosa/El Diario del Mimosa*, Llyfrgell Genedlaethol Cymru, 2000.

Agreement and Account of Crew, Official Log, Births, Marriages and Deaths, Certificates of Endorsement, BT99/230, The National Archives, Kew, Surrey.

The Welsh Colony in Patagonia, University of Bangor, Rare Book Room, BMS 78627 (AX15 GWL), pp. 90-91. (Correspondence pertaining to the first months of the colony, including letters written on board *Mimosa* to relatives in Wales and a letter, published in the *Liverpool Mercury* on January 30, 1866, by an anonymous writer, possibly Henry, the younger brother of Thomas Greene, based on an account sent to him by Thomas Greene, after he departed the colony.)

Letter from Captain Williams, concerning his refusal to furnish a ship to transport the settlers to Patagonia, *Yr Herald Cymraeg*, March 17, 1866.

Documents relating to the costs of chartering and refitting, Michael D Jones' diary, contract between Thomas Greene and Michael D Jones, cost and contents of medicine chest, etc. Bangor MSS 11456.

Brazil – history, sugar and cotton trade

Baines, Edward, *History of the Cotton Manufacture in Great Britain*, London, 1835.

Barickman, B J, *A Bahian Counterpoint 1780 to 1860, Sugar and the Underdevelopment of Northeastern Brazil,* Stanford University Press, 1998.

Peter L. Eisenberg, *The Sugar Industry in Pernambuco*, University of California Press, 1974.

Fausto, Boris, *A Concise History of Brazil*, University of Cambridge Press, 1999.

Guenther, Louise H, *British Merchants in 19th Century Brazil: business, culture and identity in Bahia, 1808-1850,* Centre for Brazilian Studies, University of Oxford, 2004.

Graham, Richard, *Britain and the Onset of Modernization in Brazil, 1850 – 1914,* Cambridge University Press, 1968.

The Palm Oil Trade

Davies, Peter N, *Trading in West Africa*, London, 1976.

Finigan, L, *The Life of Peter Stuart: the Ditton Doctor* (privately published), 1920.

Latham, A J H, *Old Calabar 1600-1891*, Oxford: Clarendon Press, 1973.

Lynn, Martin, *Commerce and Economic Change in West Africa: The Palm Oil Industry in the 19th Century*, Cambridge University Press, 1997.

Mimosa is just one of a whole range of
publications from Y Lolfa. For a full list
of books currently in print, send now
for your free copy of our new full-colour
catalogue. Or simply surf into our website

www.ylolfa.com

for secure on-line ordering.

TALYBONT CEREDIGION CYMRU SY24 5AP
e-mail ylolfa@ylolfa.com
website www.ylolfa.com
phone (01970) 832 304
fax 832 782